Introduction to "The First Draft of a Report on the EDVAC"
by John von Neumann

Michael D. Godfrey

Normally first drafts are neither intended nor suitable for publication. This report is an exception. It is a first draft in the usual sense, but it contains a wealth of information, and it had a pervasive influence when it was first written. Most prominently, Alan Turing cites it, in his Proposal for the Pilot ACE,[1] as the definitive source for understanding the nature and design of a general-purpose digital computer.

After having influenced the first generation of digital computer engineers, the von Neumann report fell out of sight. There were at least two reasons for this: The report was hard to find and it was very hard to read. This is where its first draft quality resurfaced. A draft was typed at the Moore School from von Neumann's hand written manuscript. This was subsequently edited a number of times.

The typescripts that I have used are the one held in the University of Pennsylvania Moore School and the one held in the American Philosophical Society Library (material from this copy is published by permission of the American Philosophical Society).

It is clear that the typescripts were never carefully proof read. There are numerous typographical mistakes, and serious misunderstandings about the intended use of mathematical symbols and Greek letters. There are also a considerable number of errors which may have been in the original manuscript. (Efforts to locate the manuscript have failed.)

In addition, throughout the text von Neumann refers to subsequent Sections which apparently were never written. Most prominently, the Sections on programming and on the input/output system are missing. It would have been wonderful if somehow von Neumann had found the opportunity to write those sections.

I undertook the task of carrying out a careful proof reading.[3] Initially, this was in order to fully understand the Report. However as the effort became increasingly time-consuming, I realized that the result could usefully save time and effort for others. It seemed reasonable to create a machine-readable copy and to use TeX to make the editing easier and more effective. I have taken great pains NOT to modify the intended expression, nor to editorialize on the original work. The report is still not easy reading, but to the best of my ability this version is a correct rendering of what von Neumann wrote.

A careful reading of the Report will be instructive to anyone with an interest in the past, present, or future of computing.

An earlier version of his report, without Sections 13.6 and 13.7 and the final Table found in the APS copy, has been published in: *IEEE Annals of the History of Computing*, Vol. 15, No. 4, pp.27-43, 1993.

Update Notes

On 17 November 2010, Sunit Mahajan sent an email based on a careful proofreading which found several cases deserving clarification. I have taken this opportunity to update the files in other minor ways, including hyperlinks for the Table of Contents and Figures.

---

[1] A.M. Turing, "Proposals for Development in the Mathematics Division of an Automatic Computing Engine (ACE)," presented to the National Physical Laboratory, 1945. Reprinted as Com Sci 57, National Physical laboratory, Teddington, UK, 1972.

[3] See also M.D. Godfrey and D.F. Hendry, "The Computer as von Neumann Planned It," *IEEE Annals of the History of Computing*, Vol. 15, No. 1, 1993, pp. 11-21.

In December 2012 it was brought to my attention by Mai Sugimoto[2] that additional Sections of the Report appeared in a draft copy found in the American Philosophical Society library in Philadelphia. I obtained a copy of this version and compared it with the Moore School copy. The two are nearly identical except for details of layout and pagination and the additional Sections 13.6 and 13.7 including new Figures 23 through 28, and the additional final Table which describes three planned EDVAC models. It appears that the APS draft predates the Moore School version. The two were typed on different typewriters: both versions used a typewriter without Greek letters. The Greek letter and other symbols were all written in by hand, or normal letters were used, such as t for τ. Figure 8 is correct in the APS version, but missing a connection in the Moore School version. All of the Figures were redrawn between versions. Some typos were corrected in the Moore School version and a few new ones introduced. In any case, the missing Sections 13.6 and 13.7 provide substantial new definition of the switching logic for the SG's.

September 2017

[2] See Mai Sugimoto, "On the original copies of 'First Draft of a Report on the EDVAC' by John von Neumnann," PHS Studies, No. 6, pp. 83-89, Feb 2012. At: hdl.handle.net

CONTENTS

1.0 DEFINITIONS

1

2.0 MAIN SUBDIVISIONS OF THE SYSTEM

1

3.0 PROCEDURE OF DISCUSSION

4

4.0 ELEMENTS, SYNCHRONISM NEURON ANALOGY

4

5.0 PRINCIPLES GOVERNING THE ARITHMETICAL OPERATIONS

6

CONTENTS

FIGURES

1.0 DEFINITIONS

1.1 The considerations which follow deal with the structure of a *very high speed automatic digital computing system*, and in particular with its *logical control*. Before going into specific details, some general explanatory remarks regarding these concepts may be appropriate.

1.2 An *automatic computing system* is a (usually highly composite) device, which can carry out instructions to perform calculations of a considerable order of complexity—e.g. to solve a non-linear partial differential equation in 2 or 3 independent variables numerically.

The instructions which govern this operation must be given to the device in absolutely exhaustive detail. They include all numerical information which is required to solve the problem under consideration: Initial and boundary values of the dependent variables, values of fixed parameters (constants), tables of fixed functions which occur in the statement of the problem. These instructions must be given in some form which the device can sense: Punched into a system of punchcards or on teletype tape, magnetically impressed on steel tape or wire, photographically impressed on motion picture film, wired into one or more fixed or exchangeable plugboards—this list being by no means necessarily complete. All these procedures require the use of some code to express the logical and the algebraical definition of the problem under consideration, as well as the necessary numerical material (cf. above).

Once these instructions are given to the device, it must be able to carry them out completely and without any need for further intelligent human intervention. At the end of the required operations the device must record the results again in one of the forms referred to above. The results are numerical data; they are a specified part of the numerical material produced by the device in the process of carrying out the instructions referred to above.

1.3 It is worth noting, however, that the device will in general produce essentially more numerical material (in order to reach the results) than the (final) results mentioned. Thus only a fraction of its numerical output will have to be recorded as indicated in 1.2, the remainder will only circulate in the interior of the device, and never be recorded for human sensing. This point will receive closer consideration subsequently, in particular in {12.4}.

1.4 The remarks of 1.2 on the desired automatic functioning of the device must, of course, assume that it functions faultlessly. Malfunctioning of any device has, however, always a finite probability—and for a complicated device and a long sequence of operations it may not be possible to keep this probability negligible. Any error may vitiate the entire output of the device. For the recognition and correction of such malfunctions intelligent human intervention will in general be necessary.

However, it may be possible to avoid even these phenomena to some extent. The device may recognize the most frequent malfunctions automatically, indicate their presence and location by externally visible signs, and then stop. Under certain conditions it might even carry out the necessary correction automatically and continue (cf. {3.3}).

2.0 MAIN SUBDIVISIONS OF THE SYSTEM

2.1 In analyzing the functioning of the contemplated device, certain classificatory distinctions suggest themselves immediately.

2.2 First: Since the device is primarily a computer, it will have to perform the elementary operations of arithmetics most frequently. These are addition, subtraction, multiplication and division: $+, -, \times, \div$. It is therefore reasonable that it should contain specialized organs for just these operations.

It must be observed, however, that while this principle as such is probably sound, the specific way in which it is realized requires close scrutiny. Even the above list of operations: $+, -, \times, \div$, is not beyond doubt. It may be extended to include such operation as $\sqrt{\ }$, $\sqrt[3]{\ }$, sgn, $|\ \ |$, also $\log_{10}$,

$\log_2$, ln, sin and their inverses, etc. One might also consider restricting it, e.g. omitting $\div$ and even $\times$. One might also consider more elastic arrangements. For some operations radically different procedures are conceivable, e.g. using successive approximation methods or function tables. These matters will be gone into in {10.3, 10.4}. At any rate a *central arithmetical* part of the device will probably have to exist, and this constitutes *the first specific part: CA.*

2.3 Second: The logical control of the device, that is the proper sequencing of its operations can be most efficiently carried out by a central control organ. If the device is to be *elastic*, that is as nearly as possible *all purpose*, then a distinction must be made between the specific instructions given for and defining a particular problem, and the general control organs which see to it that these instructions—no matter what they are—are carried out. The former must be stored in some way—in existing devices this is done as indicated in 1.2—the latter are represented by definite operating parts of the device. By the *central control* we mean this latter function only, and the organs which perform it form *the second specific part: CC.*

2.4 Third: Any device which is to carry out long and complicated sequences of operations (specifically of calculations) must have a considerable memory. At least the four following phases of its operation require a memory:

(a) Even in the process of carrying out a multiplication or a division, a series of intermediate (partial) results must be remembered. This applies to a lesser extent even to additions and subtractions (when a carry digit may have to be carried over several positions), and to a greater extent to $\sqrt{}$, $\sqrt[3]{}$, if these operations are wanted. (cf. {10.3, 10.4})

(b) The instructions which govern a complicated problem may constitute a considerable material, particularly so, if the code is circumstantial (which it is in most arrangements). This material must be remembered.

(c) In many problems specific functions play an essential role. They are usually given in form of a table. Indeed in some cases this is the way in which they are given by experience (e.g. the equation of state of a substance in many hydrodynamical problems), in other cases they may be given by analytical expressions, but it may nevertheless be simpler and quicker to obtain their values from a fixed tabulation, than to compute them anew (on the basis of the analytical definition) whenever a value is required. It is usually convenient to have tables of a moderate number of entries only (100–200) and to use interpolation. Linear and even quadratic interpolation will not be sufficient in most cases, so it is best to count on a standard of cubic or biquadratic (or even higher order) interpolation, (cf. {10.3}).

Some of the functions mentioned in the course of 2.2 may be handled in this way: $\log_{10}$, $\log_2$, ln, sin and their inverses, possibly also $\sqrt{}$, $\sqrt[3]{}$. Even the reciprocal might be treated in this manner, thereby reducing $\div$ to $\times$.

(d) For partial differential equations the initial conditions and the boundary conditions may constitute an extensive numerical material, which must be remembered throughout a given problem.

(e) For partial differential equations of the hyperbolic or parabolic type, integrated along a variable t, the (intermediate) results belonging to the cycle t must be remembered for the calculation of the cycle $t + dt$. This material is much of the type (d), except that it is not put into the device by human operators, but produced (and probably subsequently again removed and replaced by the corresponding data for $t + dt$) by the device itself, in the course of its automatic operation.

(f) For total differential equations (d), (e) apply too, but they require smaller memory capacities. Further memory requirements of the type (d) are required in problems which depend on given constants, fixed parameters, etc.

(g) Problems which are solved by successive approximations (e.g. partial differential equations of the elliptic type, treated by relaxation methods) require a memory of the type (e): The (intermediate) results of each approximation must be remembered, while those of the next one are being computed.

(h) Sorting problems and certain statistical experiments (for which a very high speed device offers an interesting opportunity) require a memory for the material which is being treated.

2.5 To sum up the third remark: The device requires a considerable memory. While it appeared that various parts of this memory have to perform functions which differ somewhat in their nature and considerably in their purpose, it is nevertheless tempting to treat the entire memory as one organ, and to have its parts even as interchangeable as possible for the various functions enumerated above. This point will be considered in detail, cf. {13.0}.

At any rate the total *memory* constitutes *the third specific part of the device: M.*

2.6 The three specific parts CA, CC (together C) and M correspond to the *associative* neurons in the human nervous system. It remains to discuss the equivalents of the *sensory* or *afferent* and the *motor* or *efferent* neurons. These are the *input* and the *output* organs of the device, and we shall now consider them briefly.

In other words: All transfers of numerical (or other) information between the parts C and M of the device must be effected by the mechanisms contained in these parts. There remains, however, the necessity of getting the original definitory information from outside into the device, and also of getting the final information, the results, from the device into the outside.

By the outside we mean media of the type described in 1.2: Here information can be produced more or less directly by human action (typing, punching, photographing light impulses produced by keys of the same type, magnetizing metal tape or wire in some analogous manner, etc.), it can be statically stored, and finally sensed more or less directly by human organs.

The device must be endowed with the ability to maintain the input and output (sensory and motor) contact with some specific medium of this type (cf. 1.2): That medium will be called the *outside recording medium of the device: R.* Now we have:

2.7 Fourth: The device must have organs to transfer (numerical or other) information from R into its specific parts, C and M. These organs form its *input,* the *fourth specific part: I.* It will be seen that it is best to make all transfers from R (by I) into M, and never directly into C (cf. {14.1, 15.3}).

2.8 Fifth: The device must have organs to transfer (presumably only numerical information) from its specific parts C and M into R. These organs form its *output,* the *fifth specific part: O.* It will be seen that it is again best to make all transfers from M (by O) into R, and never directly from C, (cf. {14.1, 15.3}).

2.9 The output information, which goes into R, represents, of course, the final results of the operation of the device on the problem under consideration. These must be distinguished from the intermediate results, discussed e.g. in 2.4, (e)–(g), which remain inside M. At this point an important question arises: Quite apart from its attribute of more or less direct accessibility to human action and perception R has also the properties of a memory. Indeed, it is the natural medium for long time storage of all the information obtained by the automatic device on various problems. Why is it then necessary to provide for another type of memory within the device M? Could not all, or at least some functions of M—preferably those which involve great bulks of information—be taken over by R?

Inspection of the typical functions of M, as enumerated in 2.4, (a)–(h), shows this: It would be convenient to shift (a) (the short-duration memory required while an arithmetical operation is being carried out) outside the device, i.e. from M into R. (Actually (a) will be inside the device, but in CA rather than in M. Cf. the end of 12.2). All existing devices, even the existing desk computing machines, use the equivalent of M at this point. However (b) (logical instructions) might be sensed from outside, i.e. by I from R, and the same goes for (c) (function tables) and (e), (g) (intermediate results). The latter may be conveyed by O to R when the device produces them, and sensed by I from R when it needs them. The same is true to some extent of (d) (initial conditions and parameters) and possibly even of (f) (intermediate results from a total differential equation). As to (h) (sorting and statistics), the situation is somewhat ambiguous: In many cases the possibility of using M accelerates matters decisively, but suitable blending of the use of M with a longer range use of R may be feasible without serious loss of speed and increase the amount of material that can be handled considerably.

Indeed, all existing (fully or partially automatic) computing devices use R—as a stack of punch-cards or a length of teletype tape—for all these purposes (excepting (a), as pointed out above). Nevertheless it will appear that a really high speed device would be very limited in its usefulness unless it can rely on M, rather than on R, for all the purposes enumerated in 2.4, (a)–(h), with certain limitations in the case of (e), (g), (h), (cf. {12.3}).

3.0 PROCEDURE OF DISCUSSION

3.1 The classification of 2.0 being completed, it is now possible to take up the five specific parts into which the device was seen to be subdivided, and to discuss them one by one. Such a discussion must bring out the features required for each one of these parts in itself, as well as in their relations to each other. It must also determine the specific procedures to be used in dealing with numbers from the point of view of the device, in carrying out arithmetical operations, and providing for the general logical control. All questions of timing and of speed, and of the relative importance of various factors, must be settled within the framework of these considerations.

3.2 The ideal procedure would be, to take up the five specific parts in some definite order, to treat each one of them exhaustively, and go on to the next one only after the predecessor is completely disposed of. However, this seems hardly feasible. The desirable features of the various parts, and the decisions based on them, emerge only after a somewhat zigzagging discussion. It is therefore necessary to take up one part first, pass after an incomplete discussion to a second part, return after an equally incomplete discussion of the latter with the combined results to the first part, extend the discussion of the first part without yet concluding it, then possibly go on to a third part, etc. Furthermore, these discussions of specific parts will be mixed with discussions of general principles, of arithmetical procedures, of the elements to be used, etc.

In the course of such a discussion the desired features and the arrangements which seem best suited to secure them will crystallize gradually until the device and its control assume a fairly definite shape. As emphasized before, this applies to the physical device as well as to the arithmetical and logical arrangements which govern its functioning.

3.3 In the course of this discussion the viewpoints of 1.4, concerned with the detection, location, and under certain conditions even correction, of malfunctions must also receive some consideration. That is, attention must be given to facilities for *checking* errors. We will not be able to do anything like full justice to this important subject, but we will try to consider it at least cursorily whenever this seems essential (cf. {}).

4.0 ELEMENTS, SYNCHRONISM, NEURON ANALOGY

4.1 We begin the discussion with some general remarks:

Every digital computing device contains certain relay like *elements*, with discrete equilibria. Such an element has two or more distinct states in which it can exist indefinitely. These may be perfect equilibria, in each of which the element will remain without any outside support, while appropriate outside stimuli will transfer it from one equilibrium into another. Or, alternatively, there may be two states, one of which is an equilibrium which exists when there is no outside support, while the other depends for its existence upon the presence of an outside stimulus. The relay action manifests itself in the emission of stimuli by the element whenever it has itself received a stimulus of the type indicated above. The emitted stimuli must be of the same kind as the received one, that is, they must be able to stimulate other elements. There must, however, be no energy relation between the received and the emitted stimuli, that is, an element which has received one stimulus, must be able to emit several of the same intensity. In other words: Being a relay, the element must receive its energy supply from another source than the incoming stimulus.

In existing digital computing devices various mechanical or electrical devices have been used as elements: Wheels, which can be locked into any one of ten (or more) significant positions, and which on moving from one position to another transmit electric pulses that may cause other similar wheels to move; single or combined telegraph relays, actuated by an electromagnet and opening or closing electric circuits; combinations of these two elements;—and finally there exists the plausible and tempting possibility of using vacuum tubes, the grid acting as a valve for the cathode-plate circuit. In the last mentioned case the grid may also be replaced by deflecting organs, i.e. the vacuum tube by a cathode ray tube—but it is likely that for some time to come the greater availability and various electrical advantages of the vacuum tubes proper will keep the first procedure in the foreground.

Any such device may time itself autonomously, by the successive reaction times of its elements. In this case all stimuli must ultimately originate in the input. Alternatively, they may have their timing impressed by a fixed clock, which provides certain stimuli that are necessary for its functioning at definite periodically recurrent moments. This clock may be a rotating axis in a mechanical or a mixed, mechanico-electrical device; and it may be an electrical oscillator (possibly crystal controlled) in a purely electrical device. If reliance is to be placed on synchronisms of several distinct sequences of operations performed simultaneously by the device, the clock impressed timing is obviously preferable. We will use the term *element* in the above defined technical sense, and call the device *synchronous* or *asynchronous*, according to whether its timing is impressed by a clock or autonomous, as described above.

4.2 It is worth mentioning, that the neurons of the higher animals are definitely elements in the above sense. They have all-or-none character, that is two states: Quiescent and excited. They fulfill the requirements of 4.1 with an interesting variant: An excited neuron emits the standard stimulus along many lines (axons). Such a line can, however, be connected in two different ways to the next neuron: First: In an *excitatory synapse*, so that the stimulus causes the excitation of the neuron. Second: In an *inhibitory synapse*, so that the stimulus absolutely prevents the excitation of the neuron by any stimulus on any other (excitatory) synapse. The neuron also has a definite reaction time, between the reception of a stimulus and the emission of the stimuli caused by it, the *synaptic delay*.

Following W.S. McCulloch and W. Pitts* we ignore the more complicated aspects of neuron functioning: Thresholds, temporal summation, relative inhibition, changes of the threshold by after-effects of stimulation beyond the synaptic delay, etc. It is, however, convenient to consider occasionally neurons with fixed thresholds 2 and 3, that is, neurons which can be excited only by (simultaneous) stimuli on 2 or 3 excitatory synapses (and none on an inhibitory synapse). (cf. {6.4})

It is easily seen that these simplified neuron functions can be imitated by telegraph relays or by vacuum tubes. Although the nervous system is presumably asynchronous (for the synaptic delays), precise synaptic delays can be obtained by using synchronous setups. (cf. {6.3})

4.3 It is clear that a very high speed computing device should ideally have vacuum tube elements. Vacuum tube aggregates like counters and scalers have been used and found reliable at reaction times (synaptic delays) as short as a microsecond ($= 10^{-6}$ seconds), this is a performance which no other device can approximate. Indeed: Purely mechanical devices may be entirely disregarded and practical telegraph relay reaction times are of the order of 10 milliseconds ($= 10^{-2}$ seconds) or more. It is interesting to note that the synaptic time of a human neuron is of the order of a millisecond ($= 10^{-3}$ seconds).

In the considerations which follow we will assume accordingly, that the device has vacuum tubes as elements. We will also try to make all estimates of numbers of tubes involved, timing, etc., on the basis that the types of tubes used are the conventional and commercially available ones. That is, that no tubes of unusual complexity or with fundamentally new functions are to be used. The possibilities for the use of new types of tubes will actually become clearer and more definite after a

---

* ed. Note: A logical calculus of the ideas immanent in nervous activity, *Bull. Math. Biophysics*, Vol. 5 (1943), pp. 115–133, available at: www.cs.cmu.edu.

thorough analysis with the conventional types (or some equivalent elements, cf. {}) has been carried out.

Finally, it will appear that a synchronous device has considerable advantages (cf. {6.3}).

5.0 PRINCIPLES GOVERNING THE ARITHMETICAL OPERATIONS

5.1 Let us now consider certain functions of the first specific part: The central arithmetical part CA.

The element in the sense of 4.3, the vacuum tube used as a current valve or *gate*, is an all-or-none device, or at least it approximates one: According to whether the grid bias is above or below cut-off, it will pass current or not. It is true that it needs definite potentials on all its electrodes in order to maintain either state, but there are combinations of vacuum tubes which have perfect equilibria: Several states in each of which the combination can exist indefinitely, without any outside support, while appropriate outside stimuli (electric pulses) will transfer it from one equilibrium into another. These are the so called *trigger circuits*, the basic one having two equilibria and containing two triodes or one pentode. The trigger circuits with more than two equilibria are disproportionately more involved.

Thus, whether the tubes are used as gates or as triggers, the all-or-none, two equilibrium, arrangements are the simplest ones. Since these tube arrangements are to handle numbers by means of their digits, it is natural to use a system of arithmetic in which the digits are also two valued. This suggests the use of the binary system.

The analogs of human neurons, discussed in 4.2–4.3 are equally all-or-none elements. It will appear that they are quite useful for all preliminary, orienting, considerations of vacuum tube systems (cf. {6.1, 6.2}). It is therefore satisfactory that here too the natural arithmetical system to handle is the binary one.

5.2 A consistent use of the binary system is also likely to simplify the operations of multiplication and division considerably. Specifically it does away with the decimal multiplication table, or with the alternative double procedure of building up the multiples of each multiplier or quotient digit by additions first, and then combining these (according to positional value) by a second sequence of additions or subtractions. In other words: Binary arithmetics has a simpler and more one-piece logical structure than any other, particularly than the decimal one.

It must be remembered, of course, that the numerical material which is directly in human use, is likely to have to be expressed in the decimal system. Hence, the notations used in R should be decimal. But it is nevertheless preferable to use strictly binary procedures in CA, and also in whatever numerical material may enter into the central control CC. Hence M should store binary material only.

This necessitates incorporating decimal-binary and binary-decimal conversion facilities into I and O. Since these conversions require a good deal of arithmetical manipulating, it is most economical to use CA, and hence for coordinating purposes also CC, in connection with I and O. The use of CA implies, however, that all arithmetics used in both conversions must be strictly binary. For details, cf. {11.4}.

5.3 At this point there arises another question of principle. In all existing devices where the element is not a vacuum tube the reaction time of the element is sufficiently long to make a certain telescoping of the steps involved in addition, subtraction, and still more in multiplication and division, desirable. To take a specific case consider binary multiplication. A reasonable precision for many differential equation problems is given by carrying 8 significant decimal digits, that is by keeping the relative rounding-off errors below 10^{-8}. This corresponds to 2^{-27} in the binary system, that is to carrying 27 significant binary digits. Hence a multiplication consists of pairing each one of 27 multiplicand digits with each one of 27 multiplier digits, and forming product digits 0 and 1 accordingly, and then positioning and combining them. These are essentially $27^2 = 729$ steps, and the operations of collecting and combining may about double their number. So 1000–1500 steps are essentially right.

It is natural to observe that in the decimal system a considerably smaller number of steps obtains: $8^2 = 64$ steps, possibly doubled, that is about 100 steps. However, this low number is purchased at the price of using a multiplication table or otherwise increasing or complicating the equipment. At this price the procedure can be shortened by more direct binary artifices, too, which will be considered presently. For this reason it seems not necessary to discuss the decimal procedure separately.

5.4 As pointed out before, 1000–1500 successive steps per multiplication would make any non vacuum tube device unacceptably slow. All such devices, excepting some of the latest special relays, have reaction times of more than 10 milliseconds, and these newest relays (which may have reaction times down to 5 milliseconds) have not been in use very long. This would give an extreme minimum of 10–15 seconds per (8 decimal digit) multiplication, whereas this time is 10 seconds for fast modern desk computing machines, and 6 seconds for the standard IBM multipliers. (For the significance of these durations, as well as of those of possible vacuum tube devices, when applied to typical problems, cf. {}.)

The logical procedure to avoid these long durations, consists of *telescoping operations*, that is of carrying out simultaneously as many as possible. The complexities of carrying prevent even such simple operations as addition or subtraction to be carried out at once. In division the calculation of a digit cannot even begin unless all digits to its left are already known. Nevertheless considerable simultaneisations are possible: In addition or subtraction all pairs of corresponding digits can be combined at once, all first carry digits can be applied together in the next step, etc. In multiplication all the partial products of the form (multiplicand) × (multiplier digit) can be formed and positioned simultaneously—in the binary system such a partial product is zero or the multiplicand, hence this is only a matter of positioning. In both addition and multiplication the above mentioned accelerated forms of addition and subtraction can be used. Also, in multiplication the partial products can be summed up quickly by adding the first pair together simultaneously with the second pair, the third pair, etc.; then adding the first pair of pair sums together simultaneously with the second one, the third one, etc.; and so on until all terms are collected. (Since $27 \leq 2^5$, this allows to collect 27 partial sums—assuming a 27 binary digit multiplier—in 5 addition times. This scheme is due to H. Aiken.)

Such accelerating, telescoping procedures are being used in all existing devices. (The use of the decimal system, with or without further telescoping artifices is also of this type, as pointed out at the end of 5.3. It is actually somewhat less efficient than purely dyadic procedures. The arguments of 5.1–5.2 speak against considering it here.) However, they save time only at exactly the rate at which they multiply the necessary equipment, that is the number of elements in the device: Clearly if a duration is halved by systematically carrying out two additions at once, double adding equipment will be required (even assuming that it can be used without disproportionate control facilities and fully efficiently), etc.

This way of gaining time by increasing equipment is fully justified in non vacuum tube element devices, where gaining time is of the essence, and extensive engineering experience is available regarding the handling of involved devices containing many elements. A really all-purpose automatic digital computing system constructed along these lines must, according to all available experience, contain over 10,000 elements.

5.5 For a vacuum tube element device on the other hand, it would seem that the opposite procedure holds more promise.

As pointed out in 4.3, the reaction time of a not too complicated vacuum tube device can be made as short as one microsecond. Now at this rate even the unmanipulated duration of the multiplication, obtained in 5.3 is acceptable: 1000–1500 reaction times amount to 1–1.5 milliseconds, and this is so much faster than any conceivable non vacuum tube device, that it actually produces a serious problem of keeping the device balanced, that is to keep the necessarily human supervision beyond its input and output ends in step with its operations. (For details of this cf. {}.)

Regarding other arithmetical operations this can be said: Addition and subtraction are clearly much faster than multiplication. On a basis of 27 binary digits (cf. 5.3), and taking carrying into consideration, each should take at most twice 27 steps, that is about 30–50 steps or reaction times. This amounts to .03–.05 milliseconds. Division takes, in this scheme where shortcuts and telescoping have not been attempted in multiplying and the binary system is being used, about the same number of steps as multiplication. (cf. {7.7, 8.3}). Square rooting is usually, and in this scheme too, not essentially longer than dividing.

5.6 Accelerating these arithmetical operations does therefore not seem necessary—at least not until we have become thoroughly and practically familiar with the use of very high speed devices of this kind, and also properly understood and started to exploit the entirely new possibilities for numerical treatment of complicated problems which they open up. Furthermore it seems questionable whether the method of acceleration by telescoping processes at the price of multiplying the number of elements required would in this situation achieve its purpose at all: The more complicated the vacuum tube equipment—that is, the greater the number of elements required—the wider the tolerances must be. Consequently any increase in this direction will also necessitate working with longer reaction times than the above mentioned one of one microsecond. The precise quantitative effects of this factor are hard to estimate in a general way—but they are certainly much more important for vacuum tube elements than for telegraph relay ones.

Thus it seems worthwhile to consider the following viewpoint: The device should be as simple as possible, that is, contain as few elements as possible. This can be achieved by never performing two operations simultaneously, if this would cause a significant increase in the number of elements required. The result will be that the device will work more reliably and the vacuum tubes can be driven to shorter reaction times than otherwise.

5.7 The point to which the application of this principle can be profitably pushed will, of course, depend on the actual physical characteristics of the available vacuum tube elements. It may be, that the optimum is not at a 100% application of this principle and that some compromise will be found to be optimal. However, this will always depend on the momentary state of the vacuum tube technique, clearly the faster the tubes are which will function reliably in this situation, the stronger the case is for uncompromising application of this principle. It would seem that already with the present technical possibilities the optimum is rather nearly at this uncompromising solution.

It is also worth emphasizing that up to now all thinking about high speed digital computing devices has tended in the opposite direction: Towards acceleration by telescoping processes at the price of multiplying the number of elements required. It would therefore seem to be more instructive to try to think out as completely as possible the opposite viewpoint: That of absolutely refraining from the procedure mentioned above, that is of carrying out consistently the principle formulated in 5.6.

We will therefore proceed in this direction.

6.0 E-ELEMENTS

6.1 The considerations of 5.0 have defined the main principles for the treatment of CA. We continue now on this basis, with somewhat more specific and technical detail.

In order to do this it is necessary to use some schematic picture for the functioning of the standard element of the device: Indeed, the decisions regarding the arithmetical and the logical control procedures of the device, as well as its other functions, can only be made on the basis of some assumptions about the functioning of the elements.

The ideal procedure would be to treat the elements as what they are intended to be: as vacuum tubes. However, this would necessitate a detailed analysis of specific radio engineering questions at this early stage of the discussion, when too many alternatives are still open to be treated all exhaustively and in detail. Also, the numerous alternative possibilities for arranging arithmetical procedures, logical control, etc., would superpose on the equally numerous possibilities for the choice of types and sizes of vacuum tubes and other circuit elements from the point of view of practical performance, etc. All this would produce an involved and opaque situation in which the preliminary orientation which we are now attempting would be hardly possible.

In order to avoid this we will base our considerations on a hypothetical element, which functions essentially like a vacuum tube—e.g. like a triode with an appropriate associated RLC-circuit—but which can be discussed as an isolated entity, without going into detailed radio frequency electromagnetic considerations. We re-emphasize: This simplification is only temporary, only a transient standpoint, to make the present preliminary discussion possible. After the conclusions of the preliminary discussion the elements will have to be reconsidered in their true electromagnetic nature. But at that time the decisions of the preliminary discussion will be available, and the corresponding alternatives accordingly eliminated.

6.2 The analogs of human neurons, discussed in 4.2–4.3 and again referred to at the end of 5.1, seem to provide elements of just the kind postulated at the end of 6.1. We propose to use them accordingly for the purpose described there: As the constituent elements of the device, for the duration of the preliminary discussion. We must therefore give a precise account of the properties which we postulate for these elements.

The element which we will discuss, to be called an E-element, will be represented to be a circle ◯, which receives the excitatory and inhibitory stimuli, and emits its own stimuli along a line attached to it: ◯——. This axon may branch: ◯——<, ◯——<—. The emission along it follows the original stimulation by a *synaptic delay*, which we can assume to be a fixed time, the same for all E-elements, to be denoted by τ. We propose to neglect the other delays (due to conduction of the stimuli along the lines) aside of τ. We will mark the presence of the delay τ by an arrow on the line: ◯—→, ◯—→—<. This will also serve to identify the origin and the direction of the line.

6.3 At this point the following observation is necessary. In the human nervous system the conduction times along the lines (axons) can be longer than the synaptic delays, hence our above procedure of neglecting them aside of τ would be unsound. In the actually intended vacuum tube interpretation, however, this procedure is justified: τ is to be about a microsecond, an electromagnetic impulse travels in this time 300 meters, and as the lines are likely to be short compared to this, the conduction times may indeed by neglected. (It would take an ultra high frequency device—$\tau \approx 10^{-8}$ seconds or less—to vitiate this argument.)

Another point of essential divergence between the human nervous system and our intended application consists in our use of a well-defined dispersionless synaptic delay τ, common to all E-elements. (The emphasis is on the exclusion of a dispersion. We will actually use E-elements with a synaptic delay 2τ, cf. {6.4, 7.3}.) We propose to use the delays τ as absolute units of time which can be relied upon to synchronize the functions of various parts of the device. The advantages of such an arrangement are immediately plausible, specific technical reasons will appear in { }.

In order to achieve this, it is necessary to conceive the device as synchronous in the sense of 4.1. The central clock is best thought of as an electrical oscillator, which emits in every period τ a short, standard pulse of a length τ' of about $(1/5)\tau$ – $(1/2)\tau$. The stimuli emitted nominally by an E-element are actually pulses of the clock, for which the pulse acts as a gate. There is clearly a wide tolerance for the period during which the gate must be kept open, to pass the clock-pulse without distortion. Cf. Figure 1. Thus the opening of the gate can be controlled by any electric delay device with a mean delay time τ, but considerable permissible dispersion. Nevertheless the effective synaptic delay will be τ with the full precision of the clock, and the stimulus is completely renewed and synchronized after each step. For a more detailed description in terms of vacuum tubes, cf. {}.

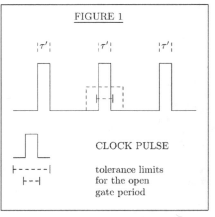

FIGURE 1

CLOCK PULSE

tolerance limits
for the open
gate period

6.4 Let us now return to the description of the E-elements.

An E-element receives the stimuli of its antecedents across excitatory synapses: —○→⊢, or inhibitory synapses: —●→⊢. As pointed out in 4.2, we will consider E-elements with thresholds 1, 2, and 3, that is, which get excited by these minimum numbers of simultaneous excitatory stimuli. All inhibitory stimuli, on the other hand, will be assumed to be absolute. E-elements with the above thresholds will be denoted by ○, ②, ③, respectively.

Since we have a strict synchronism of stimuli arriving only at times which are integer multiples of τ, we may disregard phenomena of tiring, facilitation, etc. We also disregard relative inhibition, temporal summation of stimuli, changes of threshold, changes of synapses, etc. In all this we are following the procedure of W.J. MacCulloch and W. Pitts (cf. loc. cit. 4.2). We will also use E-elements with double synaptic delay 2τ: —○→⊢→⊢, and mixed types: —○→⊲⊢.

The reason for our using these variants is that they give a greater flexibility in putting together simple structures, and they can all be realized by vacuum tube circuits of the same complexity.

It should be observed that the authors quoted above have shown that most of these elements can be built up from each other. Thus —○→⊢→⊢ is clearly equivalent to —○→⊢○→⊢, and in the case of ②→⊢ at least ☲②→⊢→⊢ is equivalent to the network of Figure 2. However, it would seem to be misleading in our application to represent these functions as if they required 2 or 3 E-elements, since their complexity in a vacuum tube realization is not essentially greater than that of the simplest E-element —○→⊢, cf. {}.

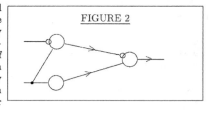

FIGURE 2

We conclude by observing that in planning networks of E-elements, all backtracks of stimuli along the connecting lines must be avoided. Specifically: The excitatory and the inhibitory synapses and the emission points—that is the three connections on ☲●→⊢ will be treated as one-way valves for stimuli—from left to right in the above picture. But everywhere else the lines and their connections ⤫ will be assumed to pass stimuli in all directions. For the delays →⊢ either assumption can be made, this last point does not happen to matter in our networks.

6.5 Comparison of some typical E-element networks with their vacuum tube realizations indicates that it takes usually 1–2 vacuum tubes for each E-element. In complicated networks, with many stimulating lines for each E-element, this number may become somewhat higher. On the average, however, counting 2 vacuum tubes per E-element would seem to be a reasonable estimate. This should take care of amplification and pulse-shaping requirements too, but of course not of the power supply. For some of the details, cf. {}.

7.0 CIRCUITS FOR THE ARITHMETICAL OPERATIONS $+, \times$

7.1 For the device—and in particular for CA—a real number is a sequence of binary digits. We saw in 5.3, that a standard of 27 binary digit numbers corresponds to the convention of carrying 8 significant decimal digits, and is therefore satisfactory for many problems. We are not yet prepared to make a decision on this point (cf. however, {12.2}), but we will assume for the time being, that the standard number has about 30 digits.

When an arithmetical operation is to be performed on such numbers they must be present in some form in the device, and more particularly in CA. Each (binary) digit is obviously representable by a stimulus at a certain point and time in the device, or, more precisely, the value 1 for that digit can be represented by the presence and the value 0 by the absence of that stimulus. Now the question arises, how the 30 (binary) digits of a real number are to be represented together. They could be represented simultaneously by 30 (possible) stimuli at 30 different positions in CA, or all 30 digits of one number could be represented by (possible) stimuli at the same point, occurring during 30 successive periods τ in time.

Following the principle of 5.6—to place multiple events in temporal succession rather than in (simultaneous) spatial juxtaposition—we choose the latter alternative. Hence a number is represented by a line, which emits during 30 successive periods τ the stimuli corresponding to its 30 (binary) digits.

7.2 In the following discussions we will draw various networks of E-elements, to perform various functions. These drawings will also be used to define *block symbols*. That is, after exhibiting the structure of a particular network, a block symbol will be assigned to it, which will represent it in all its further applications—including those where it enters as a constituent into a higher order network and its block symbol. A block symbol shows all input and output lines of its network, but not their internal connections. The input lines will be marked ⊃— and the output lines —•. A block symbol carries the abbreviated name of its network (or its function), and the number of E-elements in it as an index to the name. Cf. e.g. Figure 3 below.

7.3 We proceed to describe an *adder* network: Figure 3. The two addends come in on the input lines a', a'', and the sum is emitted with a delay 2τ against the addend inputs on the output line s. (The dotted extra input line c is for a special purpose which will appear in 8.2) The carry digit is formed by ②. The corresponding digits of the two addends together with the preceding carry digit (delay τ!) excite each one of ○ (left), ②, ③ and an output stimulus (that is a sum digit 1) results only when ○ is excited without ②, or when ③ is

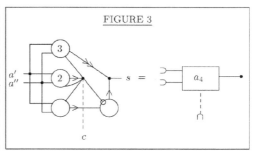

FIGURE 3

excited—that is when the number of 1's among the three digits mentioned is odd. The carry stimulus (that is a carry digit 1), results, as pointed out above, only when ② is excited—that is when there are at least two 1's among the three digits mentioned. All this constitutes clearly a correct procedure of binary addition.

In the above we have made no provisions for handling the sign of a number, nor for the positioning of its *binary point* (the analog of the *decimal point*). These concepts will be taken up in {8.0}, but before considering them we will carry out a preliminary discussion of the multiplier and the divider.

7.4 A multiplier network differs qualitatively from the adder in this respect: In addition every digit of each addend is used only once, in multiplication each digit of the multiplicand is used an many times as there are digits in the multiplier. Hence, the principle of 5.6 (cf. also the end of 7.1) requires that both factors be remembered by the multiplier network for a (relatively) considerable time: Since each number has 30 digits, the duration of the multiplication requires remembering for at least $30^2 = 900$ periods τ. In other words: It is no longer possible, as in the adder, to feed in the two factors on two input lines, and to extract in continuous operation the product on the output line—the multiplier needs a memory (cf. 2.4 (a)).

In discussing this memory we need not bring in M—this is a relatively small memory capacity required for immediate use in CA, and it is best considered in CA.

7.5 The E-elements can be used as memory devices: An element which stimulates itself, $\bigcirc\!\!\!\Rightarrow$, will hold a stimulus indefinitely. Provided with two input lines rs, cs for receiving and for clearing (forgetting) this stimulus, and with an output line os to signalize the presence of the stimulus (during the time interval over which it is remembered), it becomes the network of Figure 4.

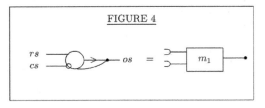

FIGURE 4

It should be noted that this $\boxed{m_1}$ corresponds to the actual vacuum tube trigger circuits mentioned at the beginning of 5.1. It is worth mentioning that $\boxed{m_1}$ contains one E-element, while the simplest trigger circuits contain one or two vacuum tubes (cf. loc. cit.), in agreement with the estimates of 6.5.

Another observation is that $\boxed{m_1}$ remembers only one stimulus, that is one binary digit. If k-fold memory capacity is wanted, then k blocks $\boxed{m_1}$ are required, or a cyclical arrangement of k E-elements: $\boxed{\bigcirc\!\!\rightarrow\bigcirc\!\!\rightarrow\!\!\rightarrow\bigcirc}$. This cycle can be provided with inputs and outputs in various ways, which can be arranged so that whenever a new stimulus (or rather the fact of its presence or absence, that is a binary digit) is received for remembering— say at the left end of the cycle—the old stimulus which should take its place—coming from the right end of the cycle—is automatically cleared. Instead of going into these details, however, we prefer to keep the cycle open: $\longrightarrow\bigcirc\!\!\rightarrow\bigcirc\!\!\rightarrow\ldots\rightarrow\bigcirc\!\!\rightarrow$

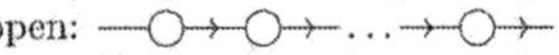

FIGURE 5

k E-elements

and provide it with such terminal equipment (at both ends, possibly connecting them) as may be required in each particular case. This simple line is shown again in Figure 5. Terminal equipment, which will normally cycle the output os at $\boxed{l_k}$'s right end back into the input at its left end, but upon stimulation at s suppress (clear) this returning of the output os and connect instead the input with the line rs, is shown in Figure 6.

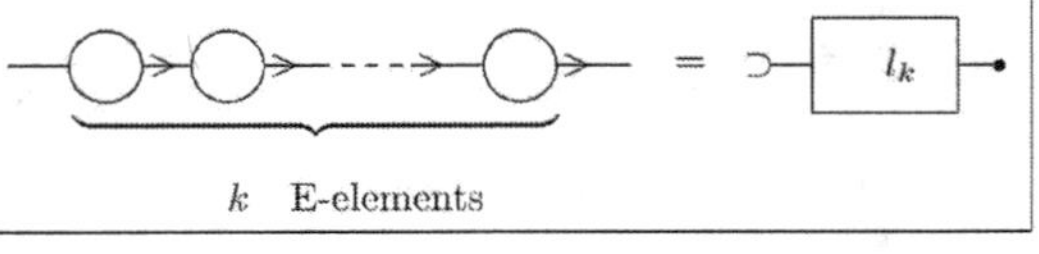

7.6 $\boxed{l_k}$, with the terminal equipment of Figure 6, is a perfect memory organ, but without it, in the form of Figure 5, it is simply a delay organ. Indeed, its sole function is to retain any stimulus for k periods t and then re-emit it and to be able to do this for successive stimuli without any interference between them.

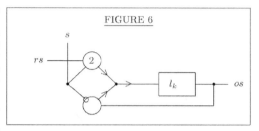

FIGURE 6

This being so, and remembering that each E-element represents (one or two) vacuum tubes, it would seem wasteful to use $k - 2k$ vacuum tubes to achieve nothing more than a delay kt. There exist delay devices which can do this (in our present situation t is about a microsecond and k is about 30) more simply. We do not discuss them here, but merely observe that there are several possible arrangements (cf. 12.5). Accordingly, we replace the block $\boxed{l_k}$ of Figure 5 by a new block $\boxed{\text{dl (k)}}$, which is to represent such a device. It contains no E-element, and will itself be treated as a new element.

We observe, that if $\boxed{\text{dl (k)}}$ is a linear delay circuit, stimuli can backtrack through it (cf. the end of 6.4). To prevent this, it suffices to protect its ends by E-elements, that is to achieve the first and the last t delay by ─○─ or to use it in some combination like Figure 6, where the E-elements of the associated network provide this protection.

7.7 We can now describe a *multiplier* network.

Binary multiplication consists of this: For each digital position in the multiplier (going from left to right), the multiplicand is shifted by one position to the right, and then it is or is not added to the sum of partial products already formed, according to whether the multiplier digit under consideration is 1 or 0.

Consequently the multiplier must contain an auxiliary network, which will or will not pass the multiplicand into the adder, according to whether the multiplier digit in question is 1 or 0. This can be achieved in two steps: First, a network is required, which will emit stimuli during a certain interval of τ periods (the interval in which the multiplicand is wanted), provided that a certain input (connected to the organ which contains the multiplier) was stimulated at

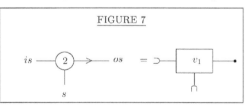

FIGURE 7

a certain earlier moment (when the proper multiplier digit is emitted). Such a network will be called a *discriminator*. Second, a valve is required which will pass a stimulus only if it is also stimulated on a second input it possesses. These two blocks together solve our problem: The discriminator must be properly controlled, its output connected to the second input of the valve, and the multiplicand routed through the valve into the adder. The valve is quite simple: Figure 7. The main stimulus is passed from *is* to *os*, the second input enters at *s*.

A *discriminator* is shown in Figure 8. A stimulus at the input {*s* and a stimulus at the input} *t* defines the moment at which the stimulus, which determines whether the later emission (at *os*) shall take place at all, must be received at the inputs. If these two stimuli coincide, the left ② is excited. Considering its feedback, it will remain excited until it succeeds in stimulating the middle ②. The middle ② is connected to ⑲ in such a manner that it can be excited by the left ② only at a moment at which ⑲ is stimulated, but at whose predecessor ⑲ was not stimulated—that is at the beginning of a sequence of stimuli at ⑲. The middle ② then quenches the left ②, and together with ⑲ excites the right ② The middle ② now becomes and stays quiescent until the end of this sequence of stimuli at ⑲ and beyond this, until the beginning of the next sequence. Hence the left ② is isolated from the two other ②, and thereby is ready to register the *s*, *t* stimuli for the next ⑲ sequence. On the other hand the feedback of the right ② is such that it will stay excited for the duration of this ⑲ sequence, and emit stimuli at *os*. There is clearly a delay 2*t* between the input at ⑲ and the output at *os*. {The connection from the output of the left ② to an input to the middle ② has been added.}

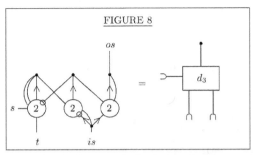

FIGURE 8

Now the *multiplier* network can be put together: Figure 9. The multiplicand circulates through ▢dl I▢, the multiplier through ▢dl II▢, and the sum of partial products (which begins with the value 0 and is gradually built up to the complete product) through ▢dl III▢. The two inputs *t*, *t'* receive the timing stimuli required by the discriminator (they correspond to *t*, *is* in Figure 8.)

FIGURE 9

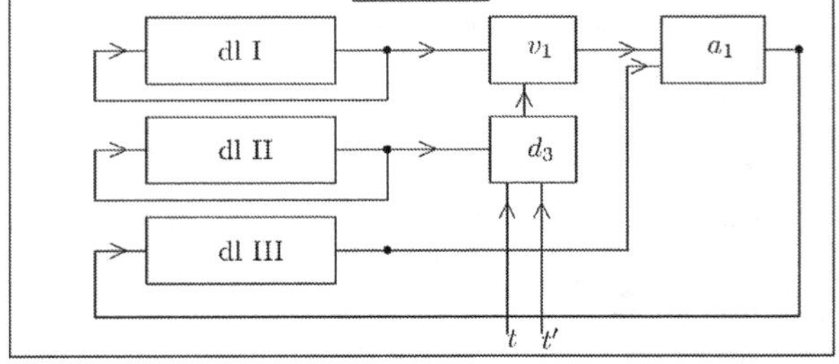

7.8 The analysis of 7.7 avoided the following essential features of the multiplier: (a) The *timing* network which controls the inputs *t*, *t'* and stimulates them at the proper moments. It will clearly have to contain ▢ dl ▢-like elements (cf. {}). (b) The *k* (delay lengths) of the ▢dl I▢ – ▢dl III▢. These too have certain functions of synchronization: Each time when the adder functions (that is in each interval *it–ft*) the multiplicand and the partial product sum (that is the outputs of ▢dl I▢ and of ▢dl III▢) must be brought together in such a manner that the former is advanced by *t* (moved by one position to the right) relatively to the latter, in comparison with their preceding encounter.

Also, if the two factors have 30 digits each, the product has 60 digits. Hence ▢dl III▢ should have about twice the *k* of ▢dl I▢ and ▢dl II▢, and a cycle in the former must correspond to about two cycles in the latter. (The timing stimuli on *t* will be best regulated in phase with ▢dl III▢.) On the other hand, it is advisable to make provisions for rounding the product off to the standard number of digits, and thereby keep the *k* of ▢dl III▢ near 30. (c) The networks required to get the multiplicand and the multiplier into ▢dl I▢ and ▢dl II▢ (from other parts of the device), and to get the product out of ▢dl III▢. (d) The networks required to handle the signs and the binary point positions of the factors. They are obviously dependent upon the way in which these attributes are to be dealt with arithmetically (cf. the end of 7.3 and {}).

All these points will be dealt with subsequently. The questions connected with (d)—arithmetical treatment of sign and binary point—must be taken up first, since the former is needed for subtraction, and hence for division too, and the latter is important for both multiplication and division.

8.0 CIRCUITS FOR THE ARITHMETICAL OPERATIONS $-$, $\div$

8.1 Until now a number x was a sequence of (about 30) binary digits, with no definition of sign or binary point. We must now stipulate conventions for the treatment of these concepts.

The extreme left digit will be reserved for the sign, so that its values 0,1 express the signs $+$, $-$, respectively. If the binary point is between the digital positions i and $i+1$ (from the left), then the positional value of the sign digit is 2^{i-1}. Hence without the sign convention the number x would lie in the interval $0 \le x < 2^{i}$, and with the sign convention the subinterval $0 \le x < 2^{i-1}$ is unaffected and corresponds to non-negative numbers, while the interval $2^{i-1} \le x < 2^{i}$ corresponds to negative numbers. We let the latter x represent a negative x', so that the remaining digits of x are essentially the complements to the digits of $-x'$. More precisely: $2^{i-1} - (-x') = x - 2^{i-1}$, that is $x' = x - 2^{i}$, for x' in the interval $-2^{i-1} \le x' < 0$.

In other words: The digital sequences which we use represent, without the sign convention, the interval $0 \le x < 2^{i}$, and with the sign convention the interval $-2^{i-1} \le x < 2^{i-1}$. The second interval is correlated to the first one by subtracting 2^{i} if necessary—that is their correspondence is modulo 2^{i}.

Since addition and subtraction leave relations modulo 2^{i} unaffected, we can ignore these arrangements in carrying out additions and subtractions. The same is true for the position of the binary point: If this is moved from i to i', then each number is multiplied by $2^{i'-i}$, but addition and subtraction leave this relation invariant too. (All these things are, of course, the analogs of the conventional decimal procedures.)

Thus we need not add anything to the addition procedure of 7.3, and it will be correct to set up a subtraction procedure in the same way. The multiplication procedure of 7.7, however, will have to be reconsidered, and the same caution applies to the division procedure to be set up.

8.2 We now set up a subtracter network. We can use the adder (cf. 7.3) for this purpose, if one addend—say the first one—is fed in the negative. According to the above this means that this addend x is replaced by $2^{i} - x$. That is each digit of x is replaced by its complement, and a unit of the extreme right digital position is then added to this addend—or just as well as an extra addend.

This last operation can be carried out by stimulating the extra input c of the adder (cf. Figure 3) at that time. This takes automatically care of all carries which may be caused by this extra addition.

The complementation of each digit can be done by a valve which does the opposite of that of Figure 7: When stimulated at s, it passes the complement of the main stimulus from is to os: Figure 10. {Note that ◯ has been relpaced by ②.}

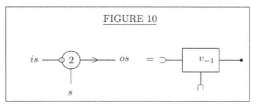

FIGURE 10

Now the *subtracter* network is shown in Figure 11. The subtrahend and the minuend come in on the input lines s, m, and the difference is emitted with a delay $3t$ against the inputs on the output line d. The two inputs t', t'' receive the necessary timing stimuli: t' throughout the period of subtraction, t'' at its first t (corresponding to the extreme right digital position, cf. above).

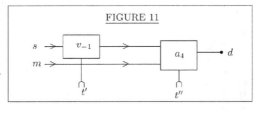

FIGURE 11

8.3 Next we form a *divider* network, in the same preliminary sense as the multiplier network of 7.7.

Binary division consists of this: For each digital position in the quotient (going from left to right), the divisor is subtracted from the partial remainder (of the dividend) already formed; but which has been shifted left by one position, preceding this subtraction. If the resulting difference is not negative (that is, if its extreme left digit is 0) then the next quotient digit is 1, and the next partial remainder (the one to be used for the following quotient digit, before the shift left referred to above) is the difference in question. If the difference is negative (that is, if its extreme left digit is 1) then the next quotient digit is 0, and the next partial remainder (in the same sense as above) is the preceding partial remainder, but in its shifted position.

The alternative in division is therefore comparable to the one in multiplication (cf. 7.7), with this notable difference: In multiplication it was a matter of passing or not passing an addend: the multiplicand. In division the question is which of two minuends to pass: the (shifted) preceding partial remainder, or this quantity minus the divisor. Hence we now need two valves where we needed one in multiplication. Also, we need a discriminator which is somewhat more elaborate than the one of Figure 8· It must not only pass a sequence of stimuli from is to os if there was a stimulus at s at the moment defined by the stimulation of t, but it must alternatively pass that sequence from is to another output os' if there was no stimulus at s at the moment in question. Comparison of Figure 8, with Figure 12 shows, that the latter possesses the desired properties. The delay between is and os or os' is now $3t$.

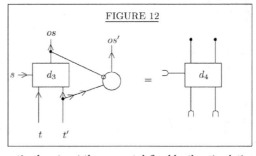

FIGURE 12

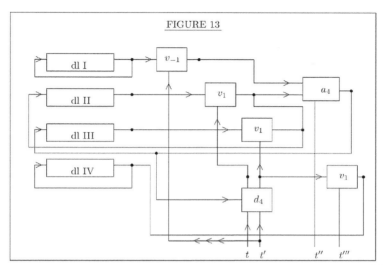

FIGURE 13

Now the *divider* network can be put together: Figure 13. The divisor circulates through $\boxed{\text{dl I}}$, while the dividend is originally in $\boxed{\text{dl III}}$, but is replaced, as the division progresses, by the successive partial remainders. The valve $\boxed{v_{-1}}$ routes the divisor negatively into the adder. The two valves $\boxed{v_1}$ immediately under it select the partial remainder (cf. below) and send it from their common output line on one hand unchanged into $\boxed{\text{dl II}}$ and on the other hand into the adder, from where the sum (actually the difference) goes into $\boxed{\text{dl III}}$. The timing must be such as to produce the required one position shift left. Thus $\boxed{\text{dl II}}$ and $\boxed{\text{dl III}}$ contain the two numbers from among which the next partial remainder is to be selected. This selection is done by the discriminator $\boxed{\text{d4}}$ which governs the two valves controlling the (second addend) input of the adder (cf. above). The resulting sum controls the discriminator, the timing stimulus at t must coincide with its appearance (extreme left digit of the sum). t' must be stimulated during the period in which the two addends (actually minuend and subtrahend) are to enter the adder (advanced by $3t$). t'' must receive the extra stimulus required in subtraction (t'' in Figure 11) coinciding with the extreme right digit of the difference. The quotient is assembled in $\boxed{\text{dl IV}}$, for each one of its digits the necessary stimulus is available at the second output of the discriminator (os' in Figure 12). It is passed into $\boxed{\text{dl IV}}$ through the lowest valve $\boxed{v_1}$, timed by a stimulus at t'''.

8.4 The analysis of 8.3 avoided the same essential features of the divider which 7.7 omitted for the multiplier, and which were enumerated in 7.8:

(a) The *timing* network which controls the inputs t, t', t'', t'''.

(b) The k (delay lengths) of the $\boxed{\text{dl I}}$ – $\boxed{\text{dl IV}}$. The details differ from those in 7.8, (b), but the problem is closely parallel.

(c) The networks required to get the dividend and the divisor into $\boxed{\text{dl III}}$ and $\boxed{\text{dl I}}$, and to get the quotient out of $\boxed{\text{dl IV}}$.

(d) The networks required to handle signs and binary point positions.

As in the case of multiplication all these points will be dealt with subsequently.

9.0 THE BINARY POINT

9.1 As pointed out at the end of 8.1, the sign convention of 8.1 as well as the binary point convention, which has not yet been determined, have no influence on addition and subtraction, but their relationship to multiplication and division is essential and requires consideration.

It is clear from the definitions for multiplication and of division, as given at the beginning of 7.7 and of 8.3 respectively, that they apply only when all numbers involved are non-negative. That is, when the extreme left digit (of multiplicand and multiplier, or dividend and divisor) is 0. Let us therefore assume this for the present (this subject will be taken up again in {}) and consider the role of the binary point in multiplication and division.

9.2 As pointed out in 7.8 (b), the product of the 30 digit numbers has 60 digits, and since the product should be a number with the same standard number of significant digits as its factors, this necessitates omitting 30 digits from the product.

If the binary point is between the digital positions i and $i + 1$ (from the left) in one factor, and between j and $j + 1$ in the other, then these numbers lie between 0 and 2^{i-1} and between 0 and 2^{j-1} (the extreme left digit is 0, cf. 9.1). Hence the product lies between 0 and 2^{i+j-2}. However, if it is known to lie between 0 and 2^{k-1} ($1 \leq k \leq i + j - 1$) then its binary point lies between k and $k + 1$. Then of its 60 digits the first $i + j - 1 - k$ (from the left) are 0 and are omitted, and so it is only necessary to omit the $29 - i - j + k$ last digits (to the right) by some rounding-off process.

This shows that the essential effect of the positioning of the binary point is that it determines which digits among the supernumerary ones in a product are to be omitted.

If $k < i+j-1$, then special precautions must be taken so that no two numbers are ever multiplied for which the product is $> 2^{k-1}$ (it is only limited by $\leq 2^{i+j-2}$). This difficulty is well known in planning calculations on IBM or other automatic devices. There is an elegant trick to get around this difficulty, due to G. Stibitz, but since it would complicate the structure of CA somewhat, we prefer to carry out the first discussion without using it. We prefer instead to suppress this difficulty at this point altogether by an arrangement which produces an essentially equivalent one at another point. However, this means only that in planning calculations the usual care must be exercised, and it simplifies the device and its discussion. This procedure, too, is in the spirit of the principle of 5.6.

This arrangement consists in requiring $k = i + j - 1$, so that every multiplication can always be carried out. We also want a fixed position for the binary point, common to all numbers: $i = j = k$. Hence $i = j = k = 1$, that is: The binary point is always between the two first digital positions (from the left). In other words: The binary point follows always immediately after the sign digit.

Thus all non-negative numbers will be between 0 and 1, and all numbers (of either sign) between -1 and 1. This makes it clear once more that the multiplication can always be carried out.

9.3 The caution formulated above is, therefore, that in planning any calculation for the device, it is necessary to see to it that all numbers which occur in the course of the calculation should always be between -1 and 1. This can be done by multiplying the numbers of the actual problem by appropriate (usually negative) powers of 2 (actually in many cases powers of 10 are appropriate, cf. {}), and transforming all formulae accordingly. From the point of view of planning it is no better and no worse than the familiar difficulty of positioning the decimal point in most existing automatic devices. It is necessary to make certain compensatory arrangements in I and O, cf. {}.

Specifically the requirement that all numbers remain between -1 and 1 necessitates to remember these limitations in planning calculations:

(a) No addition or subtraction must be performed if its result is a number not between -1 and 1 (but of course between -2 and 2).

(b) No division must be performed if the divisor is less (in absolute value) than the dividend.

If these rules are violated, the adder, subtracter and divider will still produce results, but these will not be the sum, difference, and quotient respectively. It is not difficult to include checking organs which signalize all infractions of the rules (a), (b) (cf. {}).

9.4 In connection with multiplication and division some remarks about rounding-off are necessary

It seems reasonable to carry both these operations one digit beyond what is to be kept—under the present assumptions to the 31st digit—and then omit the supernumerary digit by some rounding process. Just plain ignoring that digit would, as is well known, cause systematical rounding-off errors biased in one direction (towards 0). The usual Gaussian decimal procedure of rounding off to the nearest value of the last digit kept, and in case of a (supernumerary digit) 5 to the even one means in the binary system this: Digit pairs (30th and 31st) 00,10 are rounded to 0,1; 01 is rounded to 00; 11 is rounded by adding 01. This requires addition, with carry digits and their inconveniences. Instead one may follow the equivalent of the decimal procedure of rounding 5's to the nearest odd digit, as suggested by J. W. Mauchly. In the binary system this means that digit pairs (30th and 31st) 00, 01, 10, 11 are rounded to 0, 1, 1, 1.

This rounding-off rule can be stated very simply: The 30th digit is rounded to 1 if either the 30th or the 31st digit was 1, otherwise it is rounded to 0.

A *rounding-off valve* which does this is shown in Figure 14. A digit (stimulus) is passed from *is* to *os* while *s* is stimulated, but when *s'* is also stimulated, the digit is combined with its predecessor (that is the one to its left) according to the above rounding-off rule.

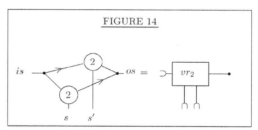

FIGURE 14

10.0 CIRCUIT FOR THE ARITHMETICAL OPERATION $\sqrt{}$. OTHER OPERATIONS

10.1 A *square rooter* network can be built so that it differs very little from the divider. The description which follows is preliminary in the same sense as those of the multiplier and the divider networks in 7.7 and 8.3.

Binary square rooting consists of this: For each digital position in the square root (going from left to right), the square root a (as formed up to that position) is used to form $2a + 1$, and this $2a + 1$ is subtracted from the partial remainder (of the radicand) already formed, but which has been shifted left by two positions (adding new digits 0 if the original digits are exhausted), before this subtraction. If the resulting difference is not negative (that is, if its extreme left digit is 0) then the next square root digit is 1, and the next partial remainder (the one to be used for the following quotient digit, before the double shift left referred to above) is the difference in question. If the difference is negative (that is, if its extreme left digit is 1) then the next square root digit is 0, and the next partial remainder (in the same sense as above) is the preceding partial remainder, but in its doubly shifted position.

This procedure is obviously very similar to that one used in division (cf. 8.3), with the following differences: First: The simple left shifts (of the partial remainder) are replaced by double ones (with possible additions of new digits 0). Second: The quantity which is being subtracted is not one given at the start (the dividend), but one that is determined by the result obtained so far: $2a + 1$ if a is the square root up to the position under consideration.

The first difference is a rather simple matter of timing, requiring no essential additional equipment. The second difference involves a change in the connection, but also no equipment. It is true, that $2a + 1$ must be formed from a, but this is a particularly simple operation in the binary system·

$2a$ is formed by a shift left, and since $2a + 1$ is required for a subtraction, the final $+1$ can be taken into account by omitting the usual correction of the extreme right digit in subtraction (cf. 8.2, it is the stimulus on t'' in Figure 11 which is to be omitted).

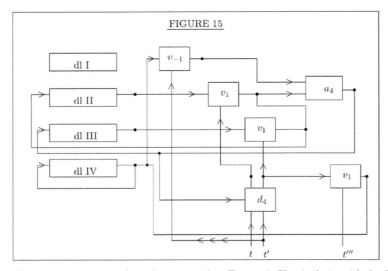

FIGURE 15

Now the *square rooter* network can be put together: Figure 15. The similarity with the divider network of Figure 13 is striking. It will be noted that $\boxed{\text{dl I}}$ is not needed. The radicand is originally in $\boxed{\text{dl III}}$, but is replaced, as the square rooting progresses, by the successive partial remainders. The valve $\boxed{v_{-1}}$ routes the square root a (as formed up to that position) negatively into the adder—the timing must be such as to produce a shift left thereby replacing a by $2a$, and the absence of the extra correcting pulse for subtraction (t'' in Figures 11 and 13, cf. the discussion above) replaces it by $2a+1$. The two valves $\boxed{v_1}$ immediately under it select the partial remainder (cf. below) and send it from their common output line on one hand unchanged into $\boxed{\text{dl II}}$ and on the other hand into the adder, from where the sum (actually the difference) goes into $\boxed{\text{dl III}}$. The timing must be such as to produce the required double position shift left. Thus $\boxed{\text{dl II}}$ and $\boxed{\text{dl III}}$ contain the two numbers from among which the next partial remainder is to be selected. This selection is done by the discriminator $\boxed{d_4}$ which governs the two valves controlling the (second addend) input of the adder (cf. the discussion of Figure 12 in 8.3). The sign digit of the resulting sum controls the discriminator. The timing stimulus at t must coincide with its appearance (extreme left digit of the sum) and t' must be stimulated during the period during which the two addends (actually minuend and subtrahend) are to enter the adder (advanced by $3t$). The square root is assembled in $\boxed{\text{dl IV}}$. For each one of its digits the necessary stimulus is available at the second output of the discriminator (os' in Figure 12). It is passed into $\boxed{\text{dl IV}}$ through the lowest valve $\boxed{v_1}$, timed by a stimulus at t'''.

10.2 The concluding remarks of 8.4 concerning the divider apply essentially unchanged to the square rooter.

The rules of 9.3 concerning the sizes of numbers entering into various operations are easily extended to cover square rooting: The radicand must be non negative and the square root which is produced will be non negative. Hence square rooting must only be performed if the radicand is between 0 and 1, and the square root will also lie between 0 and 1.

The other remarks in 9.3 and 9.4 apply to square rooting too.

10.3 The networks which can add, subtract, multiply, divide and square root having been described, it is now possible to decide how they are to be integrated in CA, and which operations CA should be able to perform.

The first question is, whether it is necessary or worth while to include all the operations enumerated above: $+, -, \times, \div, \sqrt{}$.

Little need be said about $+, -$: These operations are so fundamental and so frequent, and the networks which execute them are so simple (cf. Figures 3 and 11), that it is clear that they should be included.

With $\times$ the need for discussion begins, and at this stage a certain point of principle may be brought out. Prima facie it would seem justified to provide for a multiplier, since the operation $\times$ is very important, and the multiplier of Figure 9—while not nearly as simple as the adder of Figure 3—is still very simple compared with the complexity of the entire device. Also, it contains an adder and therefore permits to carry out $+, -$ on the same equipment as $\times$, and it has been made very simple by following the principle formulated in 5.3–5.7.

There are nevertheless possible doubts about the stringency of these considerations. Indeed multiplication (and similarly division and square rooting) can be reduced to addition (or subtraction or halving—the latter being merely a shift to the right in the binary system) by using (preferably base 2) logarithm and antilogarithm tables. Now function tables will have to be incorporated into the complete device anyhow, and logarithm-antilogarithm tables are among the most frequently used ones—why not use them then to eliminate $\times$ (and $\div, \sqrt{}$) as special operations? The answer is, that no function table can be detailed enough to be used without interpolation (this would under the conditions contemplated, require $2^{30} \approx 10^9$ entries!), and interpolation requires multiplication! It is true that one might use a lower precision multiplication in interpolating, and gain a higher precision one by this procedure—and this could be elaborated to a complete system of multiplication by successive approximations. Simple estimates show, however, that such a procedure is actually more laborious than the ordinary arithmetical one for multiplication. Barring such procedures, one can therefore state, that function tables can be used for simplifying arithmetical (or any other) operation only after the operation $\times$ has been taken care of, not before! This, then, would seem to justify the inclusion of $\times$ among the operations of CA.

Finally we come to $\div$ and $\sqrt{}$. These could now certainly be handled by function tables: Both $\div$ and $\sqrt{}$ with logarithm–antilogarithm ones, $\div$ also with reciprocal tables (and $\times$). There are also well known, fast convergent iterative processes: For the reciprocal $u \leftarrow 2u - au^2 = (2 - au)u$ (two operations $\times$ per stage, this converges to $\frac{1}{a}$), for the square root $u \leftarrow (3/2)u - 2au^3 = (3/2 - (2au)u)u$ (three operations $\times$ per stage, this converges to $\frac{1}{\sqrt{4a}}$, hence it must be multiplied by $2a$ at the end, to give $\sqrt{a}$).

However, all these processes require more or less involved logical controls and they replace $\div$ and $\sqrt{}$ by not inconsiderable numbers of operations $\times$. Now our discussions of $\times, \div, \sqrt{}$ show that each one of these operations lasts, with 30 (binary) digit numbers (cf. 7.1), on the order of $30^2 t$, hence it is wasteful in time to replace $\div, \sqrt{}$ by even a moderate number of $\times$. Besides the saving in equipment is not very significant: The divider of Figure 13 exceeds the multiplier of Figure 9 by above 50% in equipment, and it contains it as a part so that duplications are avoidable (cf. {below}). The square rooter is almost identical with the divider, as Figure 15 and its discussion show.

Indeed the justification of using trick methods for $\div, \sqrt{}$, all of which amount to replacing them by several $\times$, exists only in devices where $\times$ has been considerably abbreviated. As mentioned in 5.3–5.4 the duration of $\times$ and also of $\div$ can be reduced to a much smaller number of t than what we contemplate. As pointed out (loc. cit.), this involves telescoping and simultanising operations, and increasing the necessary equipment very considerably. We saw that such procedures are indicated in devices with elements which do not have the speed and the possibilities of vacuum tubes. In such devices the further circumstance may be important, that $\times$ can be more efficiently abbreviated than

$\div$ (cf. 5.4), and it may therefore be worth while to resort to the above mentioned procedures, which replace $\div, \sqrt{\ }$ by several $\times$. In a vacuum tube device based on the principles of 5.3–5.7 however, $\times, \div, \sqrt{\ }$ are all of the same order of duration and complication and the direct arithmetical approach to all of them therefore seems to be justified, in preference to the trick methods discussed above.

Thus all operations $+, -, \times, \div, \sqrt{\ }$ would seem to deserve inclusion as such in CA, more or less in the form of the networks of Figures 3, 9, 11, 13, 15, remembering that all these networks should actually be merged into one, which consists essentially of the elements of the divider, Figure 13. The whole or appropriate parts of this network can then be selected by the action of suitably disposed controlling E-elements, which act as valves on the necessary connections, to make it carry out the particular one among the operations $+, -, \times, \div, \sqrt{\ }$ which is desired (cf. {}). For additional remarks on specific operations and general logical control, cf. {}.

10.4 The next question is, what further operations (besides $+, -, \times, \div, \sqrt{\ }$) would be included in CA?

As pointed out in the first part of 10.3 once $\times$ is available, any other function can be obtained from function tables with interpolation. (For the details cf. {}.) Hence it would seem that beyond $\times$ (and $+, -$ which came before it), no further operations need be included as such in CA. Actually $\div, \sqrt{\ }$ were nevertheless included, and the direct arithmetical approach was used for them—but here we had the excuse that the arithmetical procedures involved had about the same duration as those of $\times$, and required an increase of only about 50% in equipment.

Further operations, which one might consider, will hardly meet these specifications. Thus the cube root differs in its arithmetical treatment essentially from the square root, as the latter requires the intermediate operation $2a + 1$ (cf. 10.1), which is very simple, particularly in the binary system while the former requires at the same points the intermediate operation $3a^2 + 3a + 1 = 3a(a+1) + 1$, which is much more complicated, since it involves a multiplication. Other desirable operations—like the logarithm, the trigonometric functions, and their inverses—allow hardly any properly arithmetical treatment. In these cases the direct approach involves the use of their power series, for which the general logical control facilities of the device must be adequate. On the other hand the use of function tables and interpolation, as suggested above is in most cases more effective than the direct power series approach.

These considerations make the inclusion of further algebraical or analytical operations in CA unnecessary. There are however some quite elementary operations, which deserve to be included for logical or organizational reasons. In order to discuss these it is necessary to consider the functioning of CA somewhat more closely, although we are not yet ready to do full justice to the viewpoints brought up in 7.8 and at the end of 10.3.

11.0 ORGANIZATION OF CA. COMPLETE LIST OF OPERATIONS

11.1 As pointed out at the end of 10.3 CA will be organized essentially as a divider, with suitable controls to modify its action for the requirements of the other operations. (It will, of course, also contain controls for the purposes enumerated in 7.8.) This implies that it will in general deal with two real number variables which go into the memory organs $\boxed{\text{dl I}}$, $\boxed{\text{dl II}}$ of the divider network of Figure 13. (These should coincide with the $\boxed{\text{dl I}}$, $\boxed{\text{dl II}}$ of the multiplier, Figure 9. The square rooter, Figure 15, needs no $\boxed{\text{dl I}}$, but it makes the same use of $\boxed{\text{dl II}}$. The adder and subtracter were not connected in Figures 3 and 11 to such memory organs, but they will have to be when the organization of CA is completed.) So we must think of CA as having two input organs, $\boxed{\text{dl I}}$ and $\boxed{\text{dl II}}$, and of course one output organ. (The latter has not been correlated with the adder and subtracter, cf. above. For the multiplier it is $\boxed{\text{dl III}}$, for the divider and square rooter it is $\boxed{\text{dl IV}}$. These things too will have to be adjusted in the final organization of CA.) Let us denote these two inputs of CA by I_{ca} and J_{ca}, and the output by O_{ca} (each of them with its attached memory organ), schematically shown in Figure 16.

Now the following complex of problems must be considered: As mentioned before, particularly in 2.5, an extensive memory M forms an essential part of the device. Since CA is the main internal operating unit of the device (M stores, CC administers, and I, O maintain the connections with the outside, cf. the analysis in 2.0.), the connections for transfers between M and CA are very important. How are these connections to be organized?

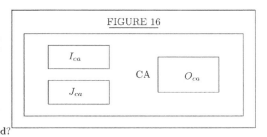

FIGURE 16

I_{ca}

J_{ca}

CA O_{ca}

It is clearly necessary to be able to transfer from any part of M to CA, i.e. to I_{ca}, J_{ca}, and conversely from CA, i.e. from O_{ca}, to any part of M. Direct connections between various parts of M do therefore not seem to be necessary: It is always possible to transfer from one part of M to the other via CA (cf. however, {14.2}). These considerations give rise to two questions: First: Is it necessary to connect each part of M with both I_{ca} and J_{ca}, or can this be simplified? Second: How are the transfers from one part of M to another part of M to be handled, where CA is only a through station?

The first question can be answered in the light of the principle of 5.6—to place multiple events in a temporal succession rather than in (simultaneous) spatial juxtaposition. This means that two real numbers which go from M into I_{ca} and J_{ca}, will have to go there in two successive steps. This being so, it is just as well to route each real number first in I_{ca}, and to move it on (within CA) from I_{ca} to J_{ca} when the next real number comes (from M) into I_{ca}. We restate:

Every real number coming from M into CA is routed into I_{ca}. At the same time the real number previously in I_{ca} is moved on to J_{ca}, and the real number previously is J_{ca} is necessarily cleared, i.e. forgotten. It should be noted, that I_{ca} and J_{ca} can be assumed to contain memory organs of the type discussed in 7.6. (cf. Figure 6, there, cf. also the various $\boxed{dl}$ in the $\times, \div, \sqrt{\ }$, networks in Figures 9, 13, 15) in which the real numbers

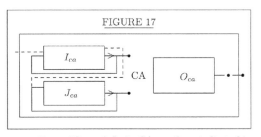

FIGURE 17

I_{ca}

J_{ca}

CA O_{ca}

they hold are circulating. Consequently the connections of I_{ca} and J_{ca} in CA are those indicated in Figure 17: The lines - - - conduct when a real number (from M) enters CA, the lines —— conduct at all other times. The connections of I_{ca} and J_{ca} with the operating parts of CA are supposed to branch out from the two terminals —•. The output O_{ca} connects with the outside (relatively to CA, i.e. with M) by the line —•—• which conducts when a result leaves CA (for M). The circulating connections of O_{ca} and its connections with the operating parts of CA are not shown, nor are the E-elements which control the connections shown (nor, of course, the operating parts of CA). (For the complete description of CA cf. {}.)

11.2 With the help of Figures 16, 17 the second question is also easily answered. For a transfer from one part of M to another part of M, going through CA, the portion of the route inside CA is clearly a transfer from I_{ca} or J_{ca} to O_{ca}. Denoting the real numbers in I_{ca}, J_{ca} by x, y, this amounts to "combining" x, y to either x or y, since the "result" of any operation performed by CA (like $+, -, \times, \div, \sqrt{\ }$) is supposed to appear at O_{ca}. This operation is trivial and a special case e.g. of addition: If x (or y) is wanted it suffices to get zero in the place of y (or x)—i.e. into I_{ca} (or J_{ca})— and then apply the operation. On the other hand, however, it seems preferable to introduce these operations as such· First: "Getting zero into I_{ca} (or J_{ca})" is unnecessarily time consuming. Second· The direct transfer from I_{ca} (or J_{ca}) to O_{ca}, which these operations require is easily effected by a small part of the CA network visualized at the beginning of 11.1. Third: We propose to introduce both operations (for I_{ca} as well as for J_{ca}), because it will appear that each can play a separate useful role in the internal administration of CA (cf. below).

We introduce accordingly two new operations: i and j, corresponding to direct transfers from I_{ca} or J_{ca} to O_{ca}.

These two operations have these further uses: It will be seen (cf. {}) that the output of CA (from O_{ca}) can be fed back directly into the input of CA (to I_{ca}, this moves the contents of I_{ca} into J_{ca} and clears J_{ca}, cf. 11.1). Now assume that I_{ca}, J_{ca} contain the real numbers x, y, and that i or j is applied, in conjunction with this feedback. Then the contents of I_{ca}, J_{ca} are replaced by (x,x) or (y,x), i.e. from the point of view of any other two variable operations $(+, -, \div$, i.e. $x + y$, $x - y$, xy, $\frac{x}{y}$) the variables x, y have been replaced by (x,x) or (y,x). Now the latter is an important manipulation for the unsymmetric operations $(x - y, \frac{x}{y})$, and the former is important for the symmetric operations $(x + y, xy)$ since it leads to doubling and squaring. Both manipulations are frequent enough in ordinary algebra, to justify a direct treatment by means of the operations i, j.

11.3 A further necessary operation is connected with the need to be able to sense the sign of a number, or the order relation between two numbers, and to choose accordingly between two (suitably given) alternative courses of action. It will appear later, that the ability to choose the first or the second one of two given numbers u, v depending upon such a relation, is quite adequate to mediate the choice between any two given alternative courses of action. (cf. {}.) Accordingly, we need an operation which can do this: Given four numbers x, y, u, v, it "forms" u if $x \geq y$ and "forms" v otherwise. (This senses the order relation between x, y. If we put $y = 0$, it senses the sign of x.)

In this form the operation has four variables: x, y, u, v. (In the sign form it has three variables: x, u, v.) Now the scheme for the CA network chosen at the beginning of 11.1, which was essentially that of the divider, had room for two variables only, and this is equally true for the discussion of the inputs of CA in 11.1. Hence four (or three) variables are too many. Consequently it is necessary to break our operation up into two variable operations—and then we might as well do this with the more general (four rather than three variables) form.

It is plausible to begin with a (partial) operation which merely decides whether $x \geq y$ or $x < y$ and remembers this, but without taking any action yet. This is best done by forming $x - y$, and then remembering its sign digit only, i.e. its first digit (from the left). (cf. 8.1. This digit is 0 for $x - y \geq 0$, i.e. $x \geq y$, and it is 1 for $x - y < 0$, i.e. $x < y$.) Thus this (partial) operation is essentially in the nature of a subtraction, and it can therefore present no additional difficulties in a CA which can subtract. Now it seems best to arrange things so that once this operation has been performed, CA will simply wait until two new numbers u, v have been moved into I_{ca}, J_{ca} (thus clearing x, y out—if u, v are to occupy I_{ca}, J_{ca}, respectively, then v must be fed in first and u second), and then transfer (without any further instructions) u or v into O_{ca} (i.e. perform i or j) according to whether the sign digit referred to above was 0 or 1.

We introduce accordingly such an operation: s. It is most convenient to arrange things so that after x, y have occupied I_{ca}, J_{ca}, a subtraction is ordered and provisions made that the result $x - y$ should remain in O_{ca}. Then x, y must be displaced from I_{ca}, J_{ca} by u, v and ordered. s will sense whether the number in O_{ca} is ≥ 0 or < 0 (i.e. $x \geq y$ or $x < y$), clear it from O_{ca}, and "form" accordingly u or v in O_{ca}. The operation preceding s need, by the way, not be subtraction: It might be addition or i or j. Accordingly the number in O_{ca}, which provides the criterion for s will not be $x - y$, but $x + y$, or $(x$ or $y)$. {missing text} i.e. s will form u or v according to whether the multiplication or the division {missing text}, and the former might indeed be sometimes useful. For details of these operations cf. {}.

11.4 Combining the conclusions of 10.2, 10.4, 11.2, 11.3 a list of eight operations of CA obtains:

$$+, -, \times, \div, \sqrt{}, i, j, s.$$

To these, two more will have to be added because of the necessity of converting numbers between the binary and the decimal systems, as indicated at the end of 5.2. Thus we need a decimal-to-binary conversion and a binary-to-decimal conversion:

$$db, bd.$$

The networks which carry out these two operations will be discussed in {Section not incl}.

This concludes for the moment the discussion of CA. We have enumerated the ten operations which it must be able to perform. The questions of 7.8, the general control problems of 11.1, and the specific networks for db, bd still remain to be disposed of. But it is better to return to these after various other characteristics of the device have been decided upon. We postpone therefore their discussion and turn now to other parts of the device.

12.0 CAPACITY OF THE MEMORY M. GENERAL PRINCIPLES

12.1 We consider next the third specific part: the memory M.

Memory devices were discussed in 7.5, 7.6, since they are needed as parts of the $\times, \div$ networks (cf. 7.4, 7.7 for $\times$, 8.3 for $\div$, 10.2 for $\sqrt{\ }$) and hence of CA itself (cf. the beginning of 11.1) In all these cases the devices considered had a *sequential* or *delay* character, which was in most cases made *cyclical* by suitable terminal organs. More precisely:

The blocks $\boxed{l_k}$ and $\boxed{dl\,(k)}$ in 7.5, 7.6 are essentially *delays*, which hold a stimulus that enters their input for a time kt, and then emit it. Consequently they can be converted into cyclical memories, which hold a stimulus indefinitely, and make it available at the output at all times which differ from each other by multiples of kt. It suffices for this purpose to feed the output back into the input: $\boxed{l_k}$ or $\boxed{dl\,(k)}$. Since the period kt contains k fundamental periods t, the capacity of such a memory device is k stimuli. The above schemes lack the proper input, clearing and output facilities, but these are shown in Figure 6. It should be noted that in Figure 6 the cycle around $\boxed{l_k}$ goes through one more E-element, and therefore the period of this device is actually $(k+1)t$, and its capacity correspondingly $k+1$ stimuli. (The $\boxed{l_k}$ of Figure 5 may, of course, be replaced by a $\boxed{dl\,(k)}$, cf. 7.6.)

Now it is by no means necessary that memory be of this cyclical (or delay) type. We must therefore, before making a decision concerning M, discuss other possible types and the advantages and disadvantages of the cyclical type in comparison with them.

12.2 Preceding this discussion, however, we must consider the *capacity* which we desire in M. It is the number of stimuli which this organ can remember, or more precisely, the number of occasions for which it can remember whether or not a stimulus was present. The presence or absence of a stimulus (at a given occasion, i.e. on a given line in a given moment) can be used to express the value 1 or 0 for a binary digit (in a given position). Hence the capacity of a memory is the number of binary digits (the values of) which it can retain. In other words:

The *(capacity) unit of memory* is the ability to retain the value of one binary digit.

We can now express the "cost" of various types of information in these memory units.

Let us consider first the memory capacity required to store a standard (real) number. As indicated in 7.1, we shall fix the size of such a number at 30 binary digits (at least for most uses, cf. {}). This keeps the relative rounding-off errors below 2^{-30}, which corresponds to 10^{-9}, i.e. to carrying 9 significant decimal digits. Thus a standard number corresponds to 30 memory units. To this must be added one unit for its sign (cf. the end of 9 2) and it is advisable to add a further unit in lieu of a symbol which characterizes it as a number (to distinguish it from an order, cf. {14.1}). In this way we arrive at $32 = 2^5$ units per number.

The fact that a number requires 32 memory units, makes it advisable to subdivide the entire memory in this way: First, obviously, into *units*, second into groups of 32 units, to be called *minor cycles.* (For the major cycles cf. {14.5}.) Each standard (real) number accordingly occupies precisely one minor cycle. It simplifies the organization of the entire memory, and various synchronization problems of the device along with it, if all other constants of the memory are also made to fit into this subdivision into minor cycles.

Recalling the classification (a)–(h) of 2.4 for the presumptive contents of the memory M, we note: (a), according to our present ideas, belongs to CA and not to M (it is handled by $\boxed{\text{dl I}}$ to $\boxed{\text{dl IV}}$, cf. the beginning of 11.1); (c)–(g), and probably (h), also consist of standard numbers; (b) on the other hand consists of the operation instructions which govern the functioning of the device, to be called *standard orders*. It will therefore be necessary to formulate the standard orders in such a manner that each one should also occupy precisely one minor cycle, i.e. 32 units. This will be done in {15.0}.

12.3 We are now in a position to estimate the capacity requirements of each memory type (a)–(h) of 2.4.

Ad (a): Need not be discussed since it is taken care of in CA (cf. above). Actually, since it requires $\boxed{\text{dl I}}$ to $\boxed{\text{dl IV}}$, each of which must hold essentially a standard number, i.e. 30 units (with small deviations, cf. {}), this corresponds to ≈ 120 units. Since this is not in M, the organization into minor cycles does not apply here, but we note that ≈ 120 units correspond to ≈ 4 minor cycles. Of course some other parts of CA are memory organs too, usually with capacities of one or a few units: e.g. the discriminators of Figures 8 and 12. The complete CA actually contains {missing text} more $\boxed{\text{dl}}$ organs, corresponding to {missing text} units, i.e. {missing text} minor cycles (cf. {}).

Ad (b): The capacity required for this purpose can only be estimated after the form of all standard orders has been decided upon, and several typical problems have been formulated—"set up"—in that terminology. This will be done in {}. It will then appear, that the capacity requirements of (b) are small compared to those of some of (c)–(h), particularly to those of (c).

Ad (c): As indicated (loc. cit.), we count on function tables of 100–200 entries. A function table is primarily a switching problem, and the natural numbers of alternatives for a switching system are the powers of 2. (cf. {}.) Hence $128 = 2^7$ is a suitable number of entries. Thus the relative precision obtained directly for the variable is 2^{-7}. Since a relative precision of 2^{-30} is desired for the result, and $(2^{-7})^4 > 2^{-30}$, $(2^{-7})^5 \ll 2^{-30}$, the interpolation error must be fifth order, i.e. the interpolation biquadratic. (One might go to even higher order interpolation, and hence fewer entries in the function table. However, it will appear that the capacity requirements of (c) are, even for 128 entries, small compared e.g. to those of (d)–(h).) With biquadratic interpolation five table values are needed for each interpolation: Two above and two below the rounded off variable. Hence 128 entries allow actually the use of 124 only, and these correspond to 123 intervals, i.e. a relative precision of 123^{-1} for the variable. However even $123^{-5} \ll 2^{-30}$ (by a factor— 2^5).

Thus a function table consists of 128 numbers, i.e. it requires a capacity of 128 minor cycles. The familiar mathematical problems hardly ever require more than five function tables (very rarely that much), i.e. a capacity of 640 minor cycles seem to be a safe overestimate of the capacity required for (c).

Ad (d): These capacities are clearly less than or at most comparable to those required by (e). Indeed the initial values are the same thing as the intermediate values of (f), except that they belong to the first value of t. And in a partial differential equation with $n + 1$ variables, say $x_1, \ldots, x_n$ and t, the intermediate values of a given t—to be discussed under (e)—as well as the initial values or the totality of all boundary values for all t correspond all three to n-dimensional manifolds (in the $n + 1$ -dimensional space) of $x_1, \ldots, x_n$ and t; hence they are likely to involve all about the same number of data.

Another important point is that the initial values and the boundary values are usually given—partly or wholly—by a formula or by a moderate number of formulae. I.e., unlike the intermediate values of (e), they need not be remembered as individual numbers.

Ad (e): For a partial differential equation with two variables, say x and t, the number of intermediate values for a given t is determined by the number of x lattice points used in the calculation. This is hardly ever more than 150, and it is unlikely that more than 5 numerical quantities should be associated with each point.

In typical hydrodynamical problems, where x is a Lagrangian label-coordinate, 50–100 points are usually a light estimate, and 2 numbers are required at each point: A position-coordinate and a velocity. Returning to the higher estimate of 150 points and 5 numbers at each point gives 750 numbers, i.e. it requires a capacity of 750 minor cycles. Therefore 1,000 minor cycles seem to be a safe overestimate of the capacity required for (e) in two variable (x and t) problems.

For a partial differential equation with three variables, say x, y and t, the estimate is harder to make. In hydrodynamical problems, at least, important progress could be made with 30 x 30 or 40 x 20 or similar numbers of x, y lattice points—say 1,000 points. Interpreting x, y again as Lagrangian labels shows that at least 4 numbers are needed at each point: Two position coordinates and two velocity components. We take 6 numbers per point to allow for possible other non hydrodynamical quantities. This gives 6,000 numbers, i.e. it requires a capacity of 6,000 minor cycles for (e) in hydrodynamical three variable (x, y and t) problems.

It will be seen (cf. {}), that a memory capacity of 6,000 minor cycles—i.e. of 200,000 units—is still conveniently feasible but that essentially higher capacities would be increasingly difficult to control. Even 200,000 units produce somewhat of an unbalance—i.e. they make M bigger than the other parts of the device put together. It seems therefore unwise to go further, and to try to treat four variable (x, y, z and t) problems.

It should be noted that two variable (x and t) problems include all linear or circular symmetric plane or spherical symmetric spatial transient problems, also certain general plane or cylinder symmetric spatial stationary problems (they must be hyperbolic, e.g. supersonic, t is replaced by y). Three variable problems (x, y and t) include all spatial transient problems. Comparing this enumeration with the well known situation of fluid dynamics, elasticity, etc., shows how important each one of these successive stages is: Complete freedom with two variable problems; extension to four variable problems. As we indicated, the possibilities of the practical size for M draw the natural limit for the device contemplated at present between the second and the third alternatives. It will be seen that considerations of duration place the limit in the same place (cf. {}).

Ad (f): The memory capacities required by a total differential equation with two variables {missing text}—i.e. to the lower estimate of (e).

Ad (g): As pointed out in (g) in 2.4, these problems are very similar to those of (e), except that the variable t now disappears. Hence the lower estimate of (e) (1,000 minor cycles) applies when a system of (at most 5) one-variable functions (of x) is being sought by successive approximation or relaxation methods, while the higher estimate of (c) (6,000 minor cycles) applies when a system of (at most 6) two-variable functions (of x, y) is being sought. Many problems of this type, however, deal with one function only—this cuts the above estimates considerably (to 200 or 1,000 minor cycles). Problems in which only a system of individual constants is being sought by successive approximations require clearly smaller capacities: They compare to the preceding problems like (f) to (e).

Ad (h): These problems are so manifold, that it is difficult to plan for them systematically at this stage.

In sorting problems any device not based on freely permutable record elements (like punchcards) has certain handicaps (cf. {}), besides this subject can only be adequately treated after an analysis of the relation of M and of R has been made (cf. 2.9 and {}). It should be noted, however, that the standard punchcard has place for 80 decimal digits, i.e. $\approx$ 9 9-digit decimal numbers, that is 9 numbers in our present sense, i.e. 9 minor cycles. Hence the 6,000 minor cycles considered in (e) correspond to a sorting capacity of $\approx$ 700 fully used cards. In most sorting problems the 80 columns of the cards are far from fully used—this may increase the equivalent sorting capacity of our device proportionately above 700. This means, that the device has a non negligible, but certainly not impressive sorting capacity. It is probably only worth using on sorting problems of more than usual mathematical complexity.

In statistical experiments the memory requirements are usually small: Each individual problem is usually of moderate complexity, each individual problem is independent (or only dependent by a few data) from its predecessors; and all that need be remembered through the entire sequence of individual problems are the numbers of how many problems successively solved had their results in each one of a moderate number of given distinct classes.

12.4 The estimates of 12.3 can be summarized as follows: The needs of (d)–(h) are alternative, i.e. they cannot occur in the same problem. The highest estimate reached here was one of 6,000 minor cycles, but already 1,000 minor cycles would permit to treat many important problems. (a) need not be considered in M. (b) and (c) are cumulative, i.e. they may add to (d)–(h) in the same problem. 1,000 minor cycles for each, i.e. 2,000 together, seem to be a safe overestimate. If the higher value 6,000 is used in (d)–(h), these 2,000 may be added for (b)–(c). If the lower value 1,000 is used in (d)–(h), it seems reasonable to cut the (b)–(c) capacity to 1,000 too. (This amounts to assuming fewer function tables and somewhat less complicated "set ups." Actually even these estimates are generous, cf. {}.) Thus total capacities of 8,000 or 2,000 minor cycles obtain.

It will be seen that it is desirable to have a capacity of minor cycles which is a power of two (cf. {}). This makes the choices of 8,000 or 2,000 minor cycles of a convenient approximate size: They lie very near to powers of two. We consider accordingly these two *total memory capacities*: $8,196 = 2^{13}$ *or* $2,048 = 2^{11}$ *minor cycles, i e.* $262,144 = 2^{18}$ *or* $65,536 = 2^{16}$ *units.* For the purposes of the discussions which follow *we will use the first higher estimate.*

This result deserves to be noted. It shows in a most striking way where the real difficulty, the main bottleneck, of an automatic very high speed computing device lies: At the memory. Compared to the relative simplicity of CA (cf. the beginning of 11.1 and {15.6}), and to the simplicity of CC and of its "code" (cf. {14 1} and {15.3}), M is somewhat impressive: The requirements formulated in 12.2, which were considerable but by no means fantastic, necessitate a memory M with a capacity of about a quarter million units! Clearly the practicality of a device as is contemplated here depends most critically on the possibility of building such an M, and on the question of how simple such an M can be made to be.

12.5 How can an M of a capacity of $2^{18} \approx 250,000$ units be built?

The necessity of introducing delay elements of very great efficiency, as indicated in 7.5, 7.6, and 12.1, becomes now obvious: One E-element, as shown in Figure 4, has a unit memory capacity, hence any direct solution of the problem of construction of M with the help of E-elements would require as many E-elements as the desired capacity of M—indeed, because of the necessity of switching and gating about four times more (cf. {}). This is manifestly impractical for the desired capacity of $\approx$ 250,000—or, for that matter, for the lower alternative in 12.4, of $\approx$ 65,000.

We therefore return to the discussion of the cyclical or delay memory, which was touched upon in 12.1. (Another type will be considered in 12.6.)

Delays $\boxed{\text{dl } (k)}$ can be built with great capacities k, without using any E-elements at all. This was mentioned in 7.6, together with the fact that even linear electric circuits of this type exist. Indeed, the contemplated t of about one microsecond requires a circuit passband of 3–5 megacycles (remember Figure 1.!) and then the equipment required for delays of 1–3 microseconds—i.e. $k = 1, 2, 3$—is simple and cheap, and that for delays up to 30–35 microseconds—i.e. $k = 30, \dots, 35$—is available and not unduly expensive or complicated. Beyond this order of k, however, the linear electric circuit approach becomes impractical.

This means that the delays $\rightarrow\!\!-$, $\rightarrow\!\!-\!\!\rightarrow\!\!-$, $\rightarrow\!\!-\!\!\rightarrow\!\!-\!\!\rightarrow\!\!-$, which occur in all E-networks of Figures 3–15 can be easily made with linear circuits. Also, that the various $\boxed{\text{dl}}$ of CA (cf. Figures 9, 13, 15, and the beginning of 11.1), which should have k values $\approx$ 30, and of which only a moderate number will be needed (cf. (a) in 12.3), can be reasonably made with linear circuits. For M itself, however, the situation is different.

M must be made up of [dl] organs, of a total capacity $\approx 250{,}000$. If these were linear circuits, of maximum capacity ≈ 30 (cf. above), then $\approx 8{,}000$ such organs would be required, which is clearly impractical. This is also true for the lower alternative of 12.4, capacity $\approx 65{,}000$, since even then $\approx 2{,}000$ such organs would be necessary.

Now it is possible to build [dl] organs which have an electrical input and output, but not a linear electrical circuit in between, with k values up to several thousand. Their nature is such, that a 4 stage amplification is needed at the output, which, apart from its amplifying character, also serves to reshape and resynchronize the output pulse. I.e. the last stage gates the clock pulse (cf. 6.3) using a non linear part of a vacuum tube characteristic which goes across the cutoff; while all other stages effect ordinary amplifications, using linear parts of vacuum tube characteristics. Thus each one of these [dl] requires 4 vacuum tubes at its output, it also requires 4 E-elements for switching and gating (cf. {}). This gives probably 10 or fewer vacuum tubes per [dl] organ. The nature of these [dl] organs is such that a few hundred of them can be built and incorporated into one device without undue difficulties—although they will then certainly constitute the greater part of the device (cf. {12.4}).

Now the M capacity of 250,000 can be achieved with such [dl] devices, each one having a capacity 1,000–2,000, by using 250–125 of them. Such numbers are still manageable (cf. above), and they require about 8 times more, i.e. 2,500–1,250 vacuum tubes. This is a considerable but perfectly practical number of tubes—indeed probably considerably lower than the upper limit of practicality. The fact that they occur in identical groups of 10 is also very advantageous. (For details cf. {}.) It will be seen that the other parts of the device of which CA and CC are electrically the most complicated, require together $\ll 1{,}000$ vacuum tubes (cf. {}). Thus the vacuum tube requirements of the device are controlled essentially by M, and they are of the order of 2,000–3,000 (cf. loc. cit. above). This confirms the conclusion of 12.4, that the decisive part of the device, determining more than any other part its feasibility, dimensions and cost, is the memory.

We must now decide more accurately what the capacity of each [dl] organ should be—within the limits which were found to be practical. A combination of a few very simple viewpoints leads to such a decision.

12.6 We saw above that each [dl] organ requires about 10 associated vacuum tubes, essentially independently of its length. (A very long [dl] might require one more stage of amplification, i.e. 11 vacuum tubes.) Thus the number of [dl] organs, and not the total capacity, determines the number of vacuum tubes in M. This would justify using as few [dl] organs as possible, i.e. of as high individual capacity as possible. Now it would probably be feasible to develop [dl]'s of the type considered with capacities considerably higher than the few thousand mentioned above. There are, however, other considerations which set a limit to increases of [dl].

In the first place, the considerations at the end of 6.3 show that the definition of [dl]'s delay time must be a fraction t' of t (about $\frac{1}{5} - \frac{1}{2}$), so that each stimulus emerging from [dl] may gate the correct clock pulse for the output. For a capacity k, i.e. a delay kt, this is relative precision $5k - 2k$, which is perfectly feasible for the device in question when $k \approx 1{,}000$, but becomes increasingly uncertain when k increases beyond 10,000. However, this argument is limited by the consideration that as the individual [dl] capacity increases correspondingly fewer such organs are needed, and therefore each one can be made with correspondingly more attention and precision.

Next there is another more sharply limiting consideration. If each $\boxed{\text{dl}}$ has the capacity k, then $\frac{250,000}{k}$ of them will be needed, and $\frac{250,000}{k}$ amplifying switching and gating vacuum tube aggregates are necessary. Without going yet into the details of these circuits, the individual $\boxed{\text{dl}}$ and its associated circuits can be shown schematically in Figure 18. Note, that Figure 6 showed the block SG in detail but the block A not at all. The actual arrangement will differ from Figure 6 in some details, even regarding SG, cf. {}. Since

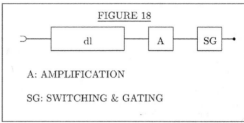

FIGURE 18

A: AMPLIFICATION

SG: SWITCHING & GATING

$\boxed{\text{dl}}$ is to be used as a memory its output must be fed back—directly or indirectly—into its input. In an aggregate of many $\boxed{\text{dl}}$ organs—which M is going to be—we have a choice to feed each $\boxed{\text{dl}}$ back into itself, or to have longer cycles of $\boxed{\text{dl}}$'s: Figure 19 (a) and (b), respectively.

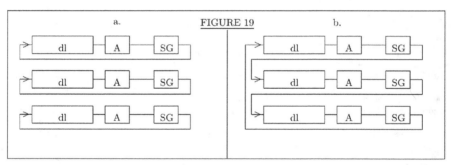

FIGURE 19

It should be noted, that (b) shows a cycle which has a capacity that is a multiple of the individual $\boxed{\text{dl}}$'s capacity—i.e. this is a way to produce a cycle which is free of the individual $\boxed{\text{dl}}$'s capacity limitations. This is, of course, due to the reforming of the stimuli traversing this aggregate at each station A. The information contained in the aggregate can be observed from the outside at every station SG, and it is also here that it can be intercepted, cleared, and replaced by other information from the outside. (For details cf. {}.) Both statements apply equally to both schemes (a) and (b) of Figure 19. Thus the entire aggregate has its inputs, outputs, as well as its switching and gating controls at the stations SG—it is here that all outside connections for all these purposes must be made.

To omit an SG in the scheme (a) would be unreasonable: It would make the corresponding $\boxed{\text{dl}}$ completely inaccessible and useless. In the scheme (b), on the other hand, all SG but one could be omitted (provided that all A are left in place): The aggregate would still have at least one input and output that can be switched and gated and it would therefore remain organically connected with the other parts of the device—the outside, in the sense used above.

We saw in the later part of 12.5, that each A and each SG required about the same number of vacuum tubes (4), hence the omission of an SG represents a 50% saving on the associated equipment at that junction.

Now the number of SG stations required can be estimated. (It is better to think in terms of scheme (b) of Figure 19 in general, and to turn to (a) only if all SG are known to be present, cf. above.) Indeed: Let each $\boxed{\text{dl}}$ have a capacity k, and let there be an SG after every l of them Then the aggregate between any two SG has the capacity $k' = kl$. (One can also use scheme (b) with aggregates of l $\boxed{\text{dl}}$'s each, and one SG each.) Hence $\frac{250,000}{k'}$ SG's are needed altogether, and the switching problem of M is a $\frac{250,000}{k'}$ way one. On the other hand every individual memory unit passes a position SG only at the end of each $k't$ period. i.e. it becomes accessible to the other parts of the device only then. Hence if the information contained in it is required in any other part of the device, it becomes necessary to wait for it—this waiting time being at most $k't$, and averaging $\frac{1}{2}k't$.

This means that obtaining an item of information from M consumes an average time $\frac{1}{2}k't$. This is, of course, not a time requirement per memory unit: Once the first unit has been obtained in this way all those which follow after it (say one or more minor cycles) consume only their natural duration, t. On the other hand this variable waiting time (maximum $k't$, average $\frac{1}{2}k't$), must be replaced in most cases by a fixed waiting time $k't$, since it is usually necessary to return to the point in the process at which the information was desired, after having obtained that information—and this amounts altogether to a precise period $k't$. (For details cf. {}.) Finally, this wait $k't$ is absent if the part of M in which the desired information is contained follows immediately upon the point at which that information is wanted and the process continues from there. We can therefore say: *The average time of transfer from a general position in M is $k't$.*

Hence the value of k' must be obtained from the general principles of balancing the time requirements of the various operations of the device. The considerations which govern this particular case are simple:

In the process of performing the calculations of mathematical problems a number in M will be required in the other parts of the device in order to use it in some arithmetical operations. It is exceptional if all these operations are linear, i.e. $+, -$; normally $\times$, and possibly $\div, \sqrt{\ }$ will also occur. It should be noted that substituting a number u into a function f given by a function table, so as to form $f(u)$, usually involves interpolation—i.e. one $\times$ if the interpolation is linear, which is usually not sufficient, and two to four $\times$'s if it is quadratic to biquadratic, which is normal. (Cf. e.g. (c) in 12.3.) A survey of several problems, which are typical for various branches of computing mathematics, shows that an average of two $\times$ (including $\div, \sqrt{\ }$) per number obtained from M is certainly not too high. (For examples cf. {}.) Hence every number obtained from M is used for two multiplication times or longer, therefore the waiting time required for obtaining it is not harmful as long as it is a fraction of two multiplication times.

A multiplication time is of the order of 30^2 times t (cf. 5 3, 7.1 and 12.2, for $\div, \sqrt{\ }$ cf 5.5) say $1,000t$ Hence our condition is that $k't$ must be a fraction of $2,000t$. Thus $k' \approx 1,000$ seems reasonable. Now a ⬚ dl ⬚ with $k \approx 1,000$ is perfectly feasible (cf. the second part of 12.5), hence $k = k' \approx 1,000$, $l = 1$ is a logical choice. In other words: Each ⬚ dl ⬚ has a capacity $k \approx 1,000$ and has an SG associated with it, as shown in Figures 18, 19.

This choice implies that the number of ⬚ dl ⬚'s required is $\approx \frac{250,000}{k} \approx 250$ and the number of vacuum tubes in their associated circuits is about 10 times more (cf. the end of 12 5), i.e. $\approx 2,500$

12.7 The factorization of the capacity $\approx 250,000$ into ≈ 250 ⬚ dl ⬚ organs of a capacity $\approx 1,000$ each can also be interpreted in this manner: The memory capacity 250,000 presents prima facie a 250,000-way switching problem, in order to make all parts of this memory immediately accessible to the other organs of the device. In this form the task is unmanageable for E-elements (e.g. vacuum tubes, cf. however 12.8). The above factorization replaces this by a 250-way switching problem, and replaces, for the remaining factor of 1,000, the (immediate, i.e. synchronous) switching by a temporal succession—i.e. by a wait of $1,000t$.

This is an important general principle: A $c = hk$-way switching problem can be replaced by a k-way switching problem and an h-step temporal succession—i.e. a wait of ht. We had $c = 250,000$ and chose $k = 1,000$, $h = 250$. The size of k was determined by the desire to keep h down without letting the waiting time kt grow beyond one multiplication time. This gave $k = 1,000$, and proved to be compatible with the physical possibilities of a ⬚ dl ⬚ of capacity k.

It will be seen, that it is convenient to have k, h, and hence also c, powers of two. The above values for these quantities are near such powers, and accordingly we choose:

Total capacity of M:	c =	262,144 =	2^{18}
Capacity of a ⬚ dl ⬚ organ:	k =	1,024 =	2^{10}
Number of ⬚ dl ⬚ organs in M:	h =	256 =	2^8

The two first capacities are stated in memory units. In terms of minor cycles of $32 = 2^5$ memory units each:

Total capacity of M in minor cycles:	c/32 =	8,192 =	2^{13}
Capacity of a ⬚ dl ⬚ organ in minor cycles:	k/32 =	32 =	2^5

12.8 The discussions up to this point were based entirely on the assumption of a delay memory. It is therefore important to note that this need not be the only practicable solution for the memory problem—indeed, there exists an entirely different approach which may even appear prima facie to be more natural.

The solution to which we allude must be sought along the lines of the *iconoscope*. This device in its developed form remembers the state of $400 \times 500 = 200,000$ separate points, indeed it remembers for each point more than one alternative. As is well known, it remembers whether each point has been illuminated or not, but it can distinguish more than two states: Besides light and no light it can also recognize—at each point—several intermediate degrees of illumination. These memories are placed on it by a light beam, and subsequently sensed by an electron beam, but it is easy to see that small changes would make it possible to do the placing of the memories by an electron beam also.

Thus a single iconoscope has a memory capacity of the same order as our desideratum for the entire M ($\approx 250,000$), and all memory units are simultaneously accessible for input and output. The situation is very much like the one described at the beginning of 12.5, and there characterized as impracticable with vacuum tube-like E-elements. The iconoscope comes nevertheless close to achieving this: It stores 200,000 memory units by means of one dielectric plate: The plate acts in this case like 200,000 independent memory units—indeed a condenser is a perfectly adequate memory unit, since it can hold a charge if it is properly switched and gated (and it is at this point that vacuum tubes are usually required). The 250,000-way switching and gating is done (not by about twice 250,000 vacuum tubes, which would be the obvious solution, but) by a single electron beam—the switching action proper being the steering (deflecting) of this beam so as to hit the desired point on the plate.

Nevertheless, the iconoscope in its present form is not immediately usable as a memory in our sense. The remarks which follow bring out some of the main viewpoints which will govern the use of equipment of this type for our purposes.

(a) The charge deposited at a "point" of the iconoscope plate, or rather in one of the elementary areas, influences the neighboring areas and their charges. Hence the definition of an elementary area is actually not quite sharp. This is within certain limits tolerable in the present use of the iconoscope, which is the production of the visual impression of a certain image. It would, however, be entirely unacceptable in connection with a use as a memory, as we are contemplating it, since this requires perfectly distinct and independent registration and storage of digital or logical symbols. It will probably prove possible to overcome this difficulty after an adequate development—but this development may be not inconsiderable and it may necessitate reducing the number of elementary areas (i.e. the memory capacity) considerably below 250,000. If this happens, a correspondingly greater number of modified iconoscopes will be required in M.

(b) If the iconoscope were to be used with $400 \times 500 = 200,000$ elementary areas (cf. above), then the necessary switching, that is the steering of the electron beam, would have to be done with very considerable precision: Since 500 elementary intervals must be distinguished in both directions of linear deflection, a minimum relative precision of $\frac{1}{2} \times \frac{1}{500} = .1\%$ will be necessary in each linear direction. This is a considerable precision, which is rarely and only with great difficulties achieved in "electrical analogy" devices, and hence a most inopportune requirement for our digital device.

A more reasonable, but still far from trivial, linear precision of, say, .5% would cut the memory capacity to 10,000 (since $100 \times 100 = 10,000$, $\frac{1}{2} \times \frac{1}{100} = .5\%$).

There are ways to circumvent such difficulties, at least in part, but they cannot be discussed here.

(c) One main virtue of the iconoscope memory is that it permits rapid switching to any desired part of the memory. It is entirely free of the octroyed* temporal sequence in which adjacent memory units emerge from a delay memory. Now while this is an important advantage in some respects, the automatic temporal sequence is actually desirable in others. Indeed, when there is no such automatic temporal sequence, it is necessary to state in the logical instructions which govern the problem precisely at which location in the memory any particular item of information that is wanted is to be found. However, it would be unbearably wasteful if this statement had to be made separately for each unit of memory. Thus the digits of a number, or more generally all units of a minor cycle should follow each other automatically. Further, it is usually convenient that the minor cycles expressing the successive steps in a sequence of logical instructions should follow each other automatically. Thus it is probably best to have a standard sequence of the constituent memory units as the basis of switching, which the electron beam follows automatically, unless it receives a special instruction. Such a special instruction may then be able to interrupt this basic sequence, and to switch the electron beam to a different desired memory unit (i.e. point on the iconoscope plate).

This basic temporal sequence on the iconoscope plate corresponds, of course, to the usual method of automatic sequential scanning with the electron beam—i.e. to a familiar part of the standard iconoscope equipment. Only the above mentioned exceptional voluntary switches to other points require new equipment.

To sum up: It is not the presence of a basic temporal sequence of memory units which constitutes a weakness of a delay memory as compared to an iconoscope memory, but rather the inability of the former to break away from this sequence in exceptional cases (without paying the price of a waiting time, and of the additional equipment required to keep this waiting time within acceptable limits, cf. the last part of 12.6 and the conclusions of 12.7). An iconoscope memory should therefore conserve the basic temporal sequence by providing the usual equipment for automatic sequential scanning with the electron beam, but it should at the same time be able of a rapid switching (deflecting) of the electron beam to any desired point under special instruction.

(d) The delay organ [dl] contains information in the form of transient waves, and needs a feedback in order to become a (cyclical) memory. The iconoscope on the other hand holds information in a static form (charges on a dielectric plate), and is a memory per se. Its reliable storing ability is, however, not unlimited in time—it is a matter of seconds or minutes. What further measures does this necessitate?

It should be noted that M's main function is to store information which is required while a problem is being solved, since the main advantage of M over outside storage (i.e. over R, cf. 2.9). Longer range storage—e.g. of certain function tables like $\log_{10}$, sin, or equations of state, or of standard logical instructions (like interpolation rules) between problems, or of final results until they are printed—should be definitely effected outside (i.e. in R, cf. 2.9 and {}). Hence M should only be used for the duration of one problem and considering the expected high speed of the device this will in many cases not be long enough to effect the reliability of M. In some problems, however, it will be too long (cf. {}), and then special measures become necessary.

The obvious solution is this: Let Nt be a time of reliable storage in the iconoscope. (Since Nt is probably a second to 15 minutes, therefore $t =$ one microsecond gives $N \approx 10^6$ - 10^9. For $N \approx 10^9$ this situation will hardly ever arise.) Then two iconoscopes should be used instead of one, so that one should always be empty while the other is in use, and after N periods t the latter should transfer

---

* ed: This is not a common term in computing then or now. Roughly it means "in the sequence determined by the grantor." Thanks to Brian Carpenter, University of Auckland, for this clarification. I had, awkwardly substituted the term "awkward" instead. November 2011

its information to the former and then clear, etc. If M consists of a greater number of iconoscopes, say k, this scheme of *renewal* requires $k+1$, and not k iconoscopes. Indeed, let $I_0, I_1, \ldots, I_k$ be these iconoscopes. Let at a given moment I_i be empty, and $I_0, \ldots, I_{i-1}, I_{i+1}, \ldots, I_k$ in use. After $\frac{N}{k+1}$ periods t, I_{i+1} should transfer its information to I_i and then clear (for $i = k$ replace $i+1$ by 0). Thus I_{i+1} takes over the role of I_i. Hence if we begin with I_0, then this process goes through a complete cycle $I_1, I_2, \ldots, I_k$ and back to I_0 in $k+1$ steps of duration $\frac{N}{k+1}t$ each, i.e. of total duration Nt. Thus all $I_0, I_1, \ldots, I_k$ are satisfactorily renewed. A more detailed plan of these arrangements would have to be based on a knowledge of the precise orders of magnitude of N and k. We need not do this here. We only wish to emphasize this point: All these considerations bring a dynamical and cyclical element into the use of the intrinsically static iconoscope—it forces us to treat them in a manner somewhat comparable to the manner in which a delay (cyclical memory) treats the single memory units.

From (a)–(d) we conclude this: It is very probable that in the end the iconoscope memory will prove superior to the delay memory. However this may require some further development in several respects, and for various reasons the actual use of the iconoscope memory will not be as radically different from that of a delay memory as one might at first think. Indeed, (c) and (d) show that the two have a good deal in common. For these reasons it seems reasonable to continue our analysis on the basis of a delay memory although the importance of the iconoscope memory is fully realized.

13.0 ORGANIZATION OF M

13.1 We return to the discussion of a delay memory based on the analysis and the conclusions of 12.6 and 12.7. It is best to start by considering Figure 19 again, and the alternatives which it exhibits We know from 12.7 that we must think in terms of $256 = 2^8$ organs $\boxed{\text{dl}}$, of capacity $1,024 = 2^{10}$ each. For a while it will not be necessary to decide which of the two alternatives, Figure 19 (a) or (b), (or which combination of both) will be used. (For the decision cf. {}.) Consequently we can replace Figure 19 by the simpler Figure 18.

The next task is, then, to discuss the terminal organs A and SG. A is a 4 stage amplifier, about which more was said in 12.5. The function of A is solely to restore the pulse emerging from $\boxed{\text{dl}}$ to the shape and intensity with which it originally entered $\boxed{\text{dl}}$. Hence it should really be considered a part of $\boxed{\text{dl}}$ proper, and there is no occasion to analyze it in terms of E-elements. SG, on the other hand, is a switching and gating organ and we should build it up from E-elements We therefore proceed to do this.

13.2 The purpose of SG is this: At those moments (i.e. periods τ) when other parts of the device (i.e. CC, CA and perhaps I, O) are to send information into the $\boxed{\text{dl}}$ to which this SG is attached, or when they are to receive information from it, SG must establish the necessary connections—at such moments we say that SG is *on*. At those moments when neither of these things is required, SG must route the output of its $\boxed{\text{dl}}$ back into the input of its (or its other) $\boxed{\text{dl}}$, according to the approximate alternative of Figure 19—at such moments we say that SG is *off*. In order to achieve this it is clearly necessary to take two lines from C (and I, O) to this SG: One to carry the $\boxed{\text{dl}}$ output to C, and one to bring the $\boxed{\text{dl}}$ input from C. Since at any given time (i.e. period τ) only one SG will be called upon for these connections with C, i.e. be on (remember the principle of 5.6!) there need only be one such pair of connecting lines, which will do for all 256 SG's. We denote these two lines by L_o and L_i, respectively. Now the scheme of Figure 18 can be made more detailed, as shown in Figure 20.

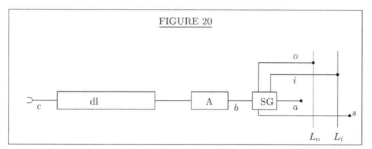

FIGURE 20

As indicated, L_o is the line connecting the outputs of all SG's to C and L_i is the line connecting C to the inputs of all SG's. When SG is off, its connections o, i with L_o, L_i are interrupted, its output goes to a, this being permanently connected to the input c of the proper $\boxed{\text{dl}}$, according to Figure 19 (a) or (b). When SG is on, its connections with a are interrupted, its output goes through o to L_o and so to C, while the pulses coming from C over L_i go into i which is now connected with a, so that these stimuli get now to a and from there to the proper $\boxed{\text{dl}}$ input (cf. above). The line s carries the stimuli which put SG on or off—clearly each SG must have its individual connection s (while L_o, L_i are common.)

13.3 Before we consider the E-network of SG, one more point must be discussed. We allowed for only one state when SG is on, whereas there are actually two: First, when SG forwards information from M to C; second, when SG forwards information from C to M. In the first case the output of SG should be routed into L_o, and also into a, while no L_i connection is wanted. In the second case L_i should be connected to a (and hence to the proper $\boxed{\text{dl}}$ input by the corresponding permanent connection of a). This information takes the place of the information already in M, which would have normally gone there (i.e. the output of SG which would have gone to a if SG had remained off), hence the output of SG should go nowhere, i.e. no L_o connection is wanted. (This is the process of *clearing*. For this treatment of clearing cf. {}) To sum up: Our single arrangement for the *on* state differs from what is needed in either of these two cases. First case: a should be connected to the output of SG, and not to L_i. Second case: a should lead nowhere, not to L_o.

Both maladjustments are easily corrected. In the first case it suffices to connect L_o not only to the organ of C which is to receive its information, but also to L_i—in this manner the output of SG gets to a via L_o, the connection of L_o with L_i. In the second case it suffices to connect L_o to nothing (except its i's)—in this manner the output of a goes into L_o, but then nowhere.

In this way the two above supplementary connections of L_o and L_i convert the originally unique *on* state of SG to be the first or the second case described above. Since only one SG is on at any one time (cf. 13.2) these supplementary connections are needed only once. Accordingly we place them into C, more specifically into CC, where they clearly belong. If we had allowed for two different *on* states of SG itself, then it would have been necessary to locate the E-network, which establishes the two corresponding systems of connections, into SG. Since there are 256 SG's and only one CC, it is clear that our present arrangement saves much equipment.

13.4 We can now draw the E-network of SG, and also the E-network in CC which establishes the supplementary connections of L_o and L_i discussed in 13.3.

Actually SG will have to be redrawn later (cf. 13.7, $pg.39$), we now give its preliminary form: SG′ in Figure 21. When s is not stimulated the two ② are impassable to stimuli, while ◯ is, hence a stimulus entering at b goes on to a, while o and i are disconnected from b and a. When s is stimulated the two ② become passable, while ◯ is blocked, hence b is now connected to o and i to a. Hence SG′ is on in the sense of 13.2 while s is stimulated, and it is off at all other times. The triple delay on ◯ is necessary for this reason:

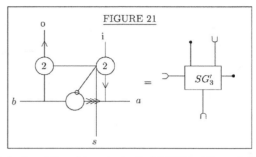

FIGURE 21

When SG′ is on, a stimulus needs one period τ to get from b to o, i.e. to L_o (cf. 13.3 and the end of this Section 13.4), and one to get from L_i, i.e. from i (cf. Figure 20) to a—that is, it takes 3τ from b to a. It is desirable that the timing should be the same when SG′ is off, i.e. when the stimulus goes via ◯ from b to a—hence a triple delay is needed on ◯.

The supplementary connections of L_o and L_i are given in Figure 22. When r is not stimulated the two ◯ are passable to stimuli; while ② is not, hence a stimulus entering at L_o is fed back into L_i and appears also at C_i, which is supposed to lead to C. When r is stimulated the two ◯ are blocked, while ② becomes passable, hence a stimulus entering at C_o, which is supposed to come from C, goes on to L_i, and L_o is isolated from all connections. Hence SCL produces the first state of 13.3 when r is not stimulated, and the second state when r is stimulated. We also note that in the first case a stimulus

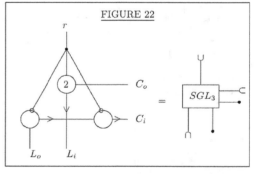

FIGURE 22

passes from L_o to L_i with a delay τ (cf. the timing question of SG′, discussed above).

13.5 We must next give our attention to the line s of Figure 20 and 21: As we saw in the first part of 13.4, it is the stimulation of s which turns SG on. Hence, as was emphasized at the end of 13.2, each SG must have its own s—i.e. there must be 256 such lines s. Turning a desired SG on, then, amounts to stimulating its s. Hence it is at this point that the $\approx$ 250-way—precisely 256-way—switching problem commented upon in 12.7 presents itself.

More precisely: It is to be expected that the order to turn on a certain SG—say No. K—will appear on two lines in CC reserved for this purpose in this manner: One stimulus on the first line expresses the presence of the order as such, while a sequence of stimuli on the second line specifies the number k desired. k runs over 256 values, it is best to choose these as $0, 1, \ldots, 255$, in which case k is the general 8-digit binary integer. Then k will be represented by a sequence of 8 (possible) stimuli on the second line, which express (by their presence or absence), in their temporal succession, k's binary digits (1 or 0) from right to left. The stimulus expressing the order as such must appear on the first line (cf. above) in some definite time relation to these stimuli on the second line—as will be seen in 13.6, $pg.37$, it comes immediately after the last digit.

Before going on, we note the difference between these 8 (binary) digit integers k and the 30 (binary) digit real numbers (lying between 0 and 1, or, with sign, between -1 and 1), the standard real numbers of 12.2. That we consider the former as integers, i.e. with the binary point at the right of the 8 digits, while in the latter the binary point is assumed to be to the left of the 30 digits, is mainly a matter of interpretation (cf. {}). Their difference in lengths, however, is material: A standard real number constitutes the entire content of a 32 unit minor cycle, while an 8 digit k is only part of an order which makes up such a minor cycle. (cf. {}.)

13.6 Let us now consider in detail the problem of switching the 256 SGs, i.e. their lines s, as circumscribed in 13.5. above. Of the two lines (in CC) introduced there, we call the first one the *signal line* and the second one the *digit line*. Our purpose is to find an E-network which does this: A stimulus on the signal line passes to the s of SG No. k, if the 8-digit binary integer k appears at the same time on the digit line. The timing of the stimuli on the signal line, the digit line, and the s line selected must be determined as a part of this process.

This switching problem can be solved in various ways. We will discuss a solution which is quite economical in the number of E-elements required, and which is a close analog of a vacuum tube arrangement that has been successfully tested in two applications. This is the *function matrix switch*. (cf.)

The function matrix switch is a 2^n-way switch, with any given $n = 1, 2, 3, \ldots$. We need it, as pointed out before, for $n = 3$. The sketches which follow will, for the sake of simplicity, be drawn for $n = 3$.

The central part of this switch is shown, in a first arrangement, in Figure 23. The stimuli coming in on the digit line [dl] go into the upper row of ◯'s, one period after the last digit of k has appeared at the left end of [dl], they occupy these ◯ in their correct order. At this time therefore each one of the upper ◯ will fire if and only if it represents a digit 1 of k. Let now a stimulus appear at this moment on the signal line sl. According to whether a certain digit of k is 1 or 0, i.e. whether the corresponding upper ◯ has or has not fired, the stimulus on sl will be able to pass the ② but not the ◯ or the ◯ but not the ② below the upper ◯ in question. Hence the impulse will pass into one and only one of the

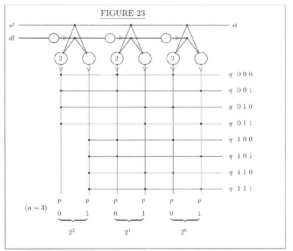

FIGURE 23

two vertical p-lines issuing from this group: 0 or 1 if the digit was 1 or 0. i.e. a p-line will carry no stimulus if and only if it represents a digit equal to the k digit in the upper ◯ of the E-element trio from which it issues. Now the connections of the horizontal q-lines with the vertical p-lines make it clear, that a -line will carry no impulse if and only the digital symbol associated with it agrees with k in all its digits–i.e. if it is the q-line No. k.

Thus the appearance of k on [dl] together with that one of a stimulus on the sl line, one period after the last digit of k, causes the appearance of stimuli on all q-lines except the q-line No. k, another period τ later.

This absence of a stimulus on the q-line in question, plus the presence of a stimulus on the sl line one period τ earlier, must be converted to a stimulus at the output of this q-line. It is also desirable that this stimulus should continue, until a new on the sl line announces the beginning of a new k-selection. This is achieved by the network of Figure 24.

Due to its feedback, this $\bigcirc$, if once excited, remains excited until it is quenched. Now a stimulus on sl, appearing on period τ after the end of k, i.e. one period before the q-lines become significantly active or inactive, will quench any previous activity of $\bigcirc$. After simple delay τ, i.e. when the q-lines become significantly active or inactive, it attempts to excite $\bigcirc$. This succeeds if and only if the q-line is inactive at this moment, i.e. if its No. is k. Thus this $\bigcirc$ and its s will become active if and only if they belong to No. k, but then they will remain active until a new stimulus on the sl line announces the beginning of a new k-selection.

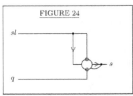

FIGURE 24

The complete 2^n-way function matrix switch thus consists of one central part, as shown on Figure 23, and of 2^n q-line terminals, as shown on Figure 24. The former contains $3n$ E-elements, the latter one E-element each, i.e. 2^n E-elements together. For our $n = 8$ these numbers are 24, and 256, i.e. 91.5% of the total 280 required are at the q-line terminals.

According to our present discussion, the central part, Figure 23, belongs to CC, while the q-line terminals, Figure 24, are associated with the SG of the same No. k. Nevertheless, it would seem to be reasonable to keep them in CC too, so that the conduction from CC to the various SG may take place on the lines s rather than on the lines q. Indeed, the SG are so numerous, that their average distance from CC must be of the order of one or more meters, while the ordinary distances within the device (e.g within C) should be of the order of centimeters, or at most decimeters. Due to the multiple connections of each q-line with its feeding p-lines and vice versa, the pulses on the q-lines are likely to be somewhat irregular, while the pulses on the s-lines come freshly from a $\bigcirc$, i.e. from the clock, and are therefore reamplified and reshaped. Consequently the s-line pulses are better suited for the journey from CC to the various SG than the q-line pulses, as asserted above.

It was pointed out by J. P. Eckert, however, that it is still better to let the p-lines be the connection from CC to the various SG. Indeed, the p-line pulses come freshly from a $\bigcirc$, i.e. from the clock, just like the q-line pulses. But since the p-lines are much fewer than the q-lines ($3n$ vs. 2^n, i.e. for n = 8, 24 vs. 256), it is much easier to provide adequate power for the CC to SG connection on the p-lines than on the q-lines.

This determines a different distribution of the organs of the function matrix switch between CC and the various SG. It implies that only the upper part of Figure 23, down to the beginning of the p-lines, inclusively, is to be in CC. The 2^n p-lines must go along all 2^n SG's, as well as the continuation of the sl-line (Figure 24). The q-line No. k in its entirety, i.e. its connections with the proper p-lines (Figure 23) as well as its terminal organs (Figure 24) belong to (and lie in the immediate vicinity of) SG No. k.

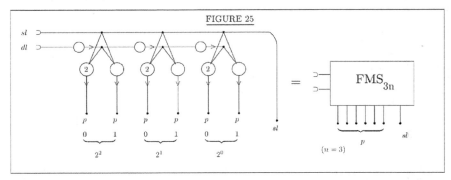

FIGURE 25

We redraw the central part of the function matrix switch accordingly: Figure 25 in place of Figure 24. The remaining parts of Figures 23 and 24, i.e. each q-line in its entirety, as described above, must be added to the corresponding SG. Actually we considered the sketch of SG in Figure

21 as preliminary, and called it SG^1. What we propose to treat as the complete and true SG consists of this SG^1, together with its q-line, etc. This is shown in Figure 26. After comparison with Figures 21, 23, and 24 this Figure 26 requires no further explanation.

13.7 With the block symbol of Figure 26, the scheme of Figures 18 and 20 for an individual ⌷ dl ⌷ and its associated circuits can be made quite precise, as shown on Figure 27.

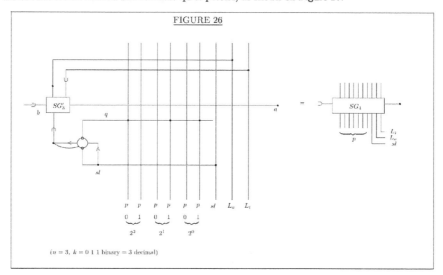

FIGURE 26

$(n = 3, \ k = 0\ 1\ 1 \text{ binary} = 3 \text{ decimal})$

The input and output ⊃— and —• at the left end of DLA correspond to the ⊃— and —• of Figures 18, 23 (a and c of Figure 20), they can be connected up in various ways, as shown by the alternatives of Figure 19.—but at any rate DLA can only function if the circuits are closed in some way between these ⊃— and —• .

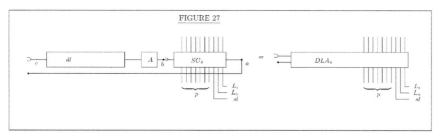

FIGURE 27

Figure 27 permits us to draw the E-network for the entire M and its connections with CC. Before doing this, however, we make two more observations.

First: As Figure 27 shows, there go through each DLA all p-lines, plus the lines sl, L_o, L_1. There are 2n p-lines, the drawing shows n = 3, i.e. 6 p-lines, but actually we have n= 8, i.e. 16 p-lines. This makes a total of *19 lines, which go through all 256 DLA organs, and connect these with each other and with CC.*

Second: We call these 19 lines the *main trunk of M.* Instead of indicating these 19 lines (or, in the simplified version of Figures 25, 26, 27, 9 lines) separately, we use a single symbol for the entire main trunk:

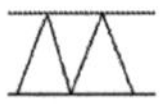

We now combine Figures 22, 25, 23 to draw the entire M and its connections with CC: Figure 28. After the exhaustive comments connected with the three underlying Figures, Figure 28 requires no detailed explanation. The following remarks, however, may be in order:

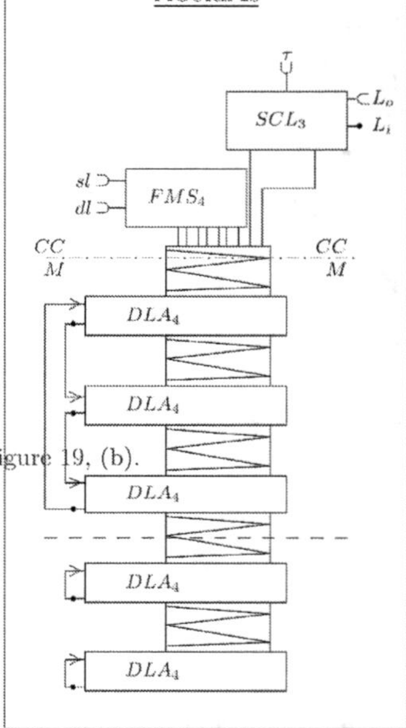

First: The part below the line $-\cdot-\cdot-\cdot$ is M. and it exhausts M. The part above that line belongs to CC, but does, of course, not exhaust it. Second: Of the 256 DLA organs only the three first and the two last are shown, the line $-\,-\,-$ indicating the omitted portion. Third: As mentioned previously, a DLA organ can only function if the $\supset$— and —● on its left end are properly connected up. On the present Figure these connections are established in two typical ways: On the two last DLA organs the $\supset$— and —● of every unit are connected to each other, thereby making each unit a closed cycle. This corresponds to the arrangement of Figure 19, (a). On the three first DLA organs their $\supset$— and —● are connected cyclically, so as to make the three units together one cycle. This corresponds to the arrangement of Figure 19, (b).

FIGURE 28

The following decisions remain to be made: Which of the two above arrangements, or which combination of both, should be used throughout M? Should the arrangement which is selected be wired in a permanent form into the actual device, or should it be possible to change some or all of these connections, with certain limits or unrestrictedly? If changes are possible should they be made by manual plugging, or by relays which may be controlled by manual switches or by punched cards or tape, or electronically? Should control by the operating device itself be envisaged? These decisions will be made successively, as the discussion of the logical control of the device progresses, specifically in (cf.).

14.0 CC AND M

14.1 Our next aim is to go deeper into the analysis of CC. Such an analysis, however, is dependent upon a precise knowledge of the system of orders used in controlling the device, since the function of CC is to receive these orders, to interpret them, and then either to carry them out, or to stimulate properly those organs which will carry them out. It is therefore our immediate task to provide a list of the orders which control the device, i.e. to describe the *code* to be used in the device, and to define the mathematical and logical meaning and the operational significance of its *code words*.

Before we can formulate this code, we must go through some general considerations concerning the functions of CC and its relation to M.

The orders which are received by CC come from M, i.e. from the same place where the numerical material is stored. (Cf. 2.4 and 12.3 in particular (b).) The content of M consists of minor cycles (cf. 12.2 and 12.7), hence by the above each minor cycle must contain a distinguishing mark which indicates whether it is a standard number or an order.

The orders which CC receives fall naturally into these four classes: (a) orders for CC to instruct CA to carry out one of its ten specific operations (cf. 11.4); (b) orders for CC to cause the transfer of a standard number from one place to another; (c) orders for CC to transfer its own connection with M to a different point in M, with the purpose of getting its next order from there; (d) orders controlling the operation of the input and the output of the device (i.e. I of 2.7 and O of 2.8).

Let us now consider these classes (a)–(d) separately. We cannot at this time add anything to the statements of 11.4 concerning (a) (cf. however {}). The discussion of (d) is also better delayed (cf. {}). We propose, however, to discuss (b) and (c) now.

14.2 Ad (b): These transfers can occur within M, or within CA, or between M and CA. The first kind can always be replaced by two operations of the last kind, i.e. all transfers within M can be routed through CA. We propose to do this, since this is in accord with the general principle of 5.6 (cf. also the discussion of the second question in 11.1), and in this way we eliminate all transfers of the first kind. Transfers of the second kind are obviously handled by the operating controls of CA. Hence those of the last kind alone remain. They fall obviously into two classes: Transfers from M to CA and transfers from CA to M. We may break up accordingly (b) into (b') and (b''), corresponding to these two operations.

14.3 Ad (c): In principle CC should be instructed, after each order, where to find the next order that it is to carry out. We saw, however, that this is undesirable per se, and that it should be reserved for exceptional occasions, while as a normal routine CC should obey the orders in the temporal sequence in which they naturally appear at the output of the DLA organ to which CC is connected. (cf. the corresponding discussion for the iconoscope memory, (c) in 12.8.) There must, however, be orders available, which may be used at the exceptional occasions referred to, to instruct CC to transfer its connection to any other desired point in M. This is primarily a transfer of this connection to a different DLA organ (i.e. a ⬚ dl ⬚ organ in the sense of 12.7). Since, however, the connection actually wanted must be with a definite minor cycle, the order in question must consist of two instructions: First, the connection of CC is to be transferred to a definite DLA organ. Second, CC is to wait there until a definite τ-period, the one in which the desired minor cycle appears at the output of this DLA, and CC is to accept an order at this time only.

Apart from this, such a transfer order might provide that, after receiving and carrying out the order in the desired minor cycle, CC should return its connection to the DLA organ which contains the minor cycle that follows upon the one containing the transfer order, wait until this minor cycle appears at the output, and then continue to accept orders from there on in the natural temporal sequence. Alternatively, after receiving and carrying out the order in the desired minor cycle, CC should continue with that connection, and accept orders from there on in the natural temporal sequence. It is convenient to call a transfer of the first type a *transient* one, and one of the second type a *permanent* one.

It is clear that permanent transfers are frequently needed, hence the second type is certainly necessary. Transient transfers are undoubtedly required in connection with transferring standard numbers (orders (c') and (c'')), cf. the end of 14.2 and in more detail in 14.4 below). It seems very doubtful whether they are ever needed in true orders, particularly since such orders constitute only a small part of the contents of M (cf. (b) in 12.3), and a transient transfer order can always be expressed by two permanent transfer orders. We will therefore make all transfers permanent, except those connected with transferring standard numbers, as indicated above.

14.4 Ad (b) again: Such a transfer between CA and a definite minor cycle in M (in either direction, corresponding to (b') or (b''), cf. the end of 14.2) is similar to a transfer affecting CC in the sense of (c), since it requires establishing a connection with the desired DLA organ, and then waiting for the appearance of the desired minor cycle at the output. Indeed, since only one connection between M and CC (actually CC or CA, i.e. C) is possible at one time, such a number transfer requires abandoning the present connection of CC with M, and then establishing a new connection, exactly as if a transfer affecting CC in the sense of (c) were intended. Since, however, actually no such transfer of CC is desired, the connection of CC with its original DLA organ must be reestablished, after the number transfer has been carried out, and the waiting for the proper minor cycle (that one following in the natural temporal sequence upon the transfer order) is also necessary. I.e. this is a transient transfer, as indicated at the end of 14.3.

It should be noted that during a transient transfer the place of the minor cycle which contained the transfer order must be remembered, since CC will have to return to its successor. I.e. CC must be able to remember the number of the DLA organ which contains this minor cycle, and the number of τ periods after which the minor cycle will appear at the output. (cf. for details {}.)

14.5 Some further remarks:

First: Every permanent transfer involves waiting for the desired minor cycle, i.e. on the average for half a transit through a DLA organ, 512 periods τ. A transient transfer involves two such waiting periods, which add up exactly to one transit through a DLA organ, 1,024 periods τ. One might shorten certain transient transfers by appropriate timing tricks, but this seems inadvisable, at least at this stage of the discussion, since the switching operation itself (i.e. changing the connection of CC) may consume a nonnegligible fraction of a minor cycle and may therefore interfere with the timing.

Second: It is sometimes desirable to make a transfer from M to CA, or conversely, without any waiting time. In this case the minor cycle in M, which is involved in this transfer, should be the one immediately following (in time and in the same DLA organ) upon the one containing the transfer order. This obviously calls for an extra type of immediate transfer in addition to the two types introduced in 14.3. This type will be discussed more fully in {15.3}.

Third: The 256 DLA organs have numbers $0, 1, \ldots, 255$, i.e. all 8-digit binary numbers. It is desirable to give the 32 minor cycles in each DLA organ equally fixed numbers $0, 1, \ldots, 31$ i.e. all 5-digit binary numbers. Now the DLA organs are definite physical objects, hence their enumeration offers no difficulties. The minor cycles in a given DLA organ, on the other hand, are merely moving loci, at which certain combinations of 32 possible stimuli may be located. Alternatively, looking at the situation at the output end of the DLA organ, a minor cycle is a sequence of 32 periods τ, this sequence being considered to be periodically returning after every 1,024 periods τ. One might say that a minor cycle is a 32τ "hour" of a $1,024\tau$ "day," the "day" thus having 32 "hours." It is now convenient to fix one of these "hours," i.e. minor cycles, as zero or {"first"} and let it be at the same time at the outputs of all 256 DLA organs of M. We can then attribute each "hour", i.e. minor cycle, its number $0, 1, \ldots, 31$, by counting from there. We assume accordingly that such a convention is established—noting that the minor cycles of any given number appear at the same time at the outputs of all 256 DLA organs of M.

Thus each DLA organ has now a number $\mu = 0, 1, \ldots, 255$ (or 8-digit binary), and each minor cycle in it has a number $\rho = 0, 1, \ldots, 31$ (or 5-digit binary). A minor cycle is completely defined within M by specifying both numbers μ, ρ. Due to these relationships we propose to call a DLA organ a *major cycle*.

Fourth: As the contents of a minor cycle make their transit across a DLA organ, i.e. a major cycle, the minor cycles number ρ clearly remains the same. When it reaches the output and is then cycled back into the input of a major cycle the number ρ is still not changed (since it will reach the output again after 1,024 periods τ, and we have synchronism in all DLA organs, and a 1,024 τ periodicity, cf. above), but μ changes to the number of the new major cycle. For individual cycling, the arrangement of Figure 19 (a), this means that μ, too, remains unchanged. For serial cycling, the arrangement of Figure 19 (b), this means that μ usually increases by 1, except that at the end of such a series of, say, s major cycles it decreases by $s - 1$.

These observations about the fate of a minor cycle after it has appeared at the output of its major cycle apply as such when that major cycle is undisturbed, i.e. when it is off in the sense of 13.2. When it is on, in the same sense, but in the first case of 13.3, then our observations are obviously still valid—i.e. they hold as long as the minor cycle is not being cleared. When it is being cleared, i.e. in the second case of 13.3, then those observations apply to the minor cycle which replaces the one that has been cleared.

15.0 THE CODE

15.1 The considerations of 14.0 provide the basis for a complete classification of the contents of M, i.e. they enumerate a system of successive disjunctions which give together this classification. This classification will put us into the position to formulate the code which effects the logical control of CC, and hence of the entire device.

Let us therefore restate the pertinent definitions and disjunctions.

The contents of M are the memory units, each one being characterized by the presence or absence of a stimulus. It can be used to represent accordingly the binary digit 1 or 0, and we will at any rate designate its content by the binary digit $i = 1$ or 0 to which it corresponds in this manner. (cf. 12.2 and 12.5 with 7.6.) These units are grouped together to form 32-unit minor cycles, and these minor cycles are the entities which will acquire direct significance in the code which we will introduce. (cf. 12.2.) We denote the binary digits which make up the 32 units of a minor cycle, in their natural temporal sequence, by $i_0, i_1, i_2, \ldots, i_{31}$. The minor cycles with these units may be written $I = (i_0, i_1, i_2, \ldots, i_{31}) = (i_v)$.

Minor cycles fall into two classes: *Standard numbers* and *orders*. (cf 12.2 and 14.1.) These two categories should be distinguished from each other by their respective first units (cf. 12.2) i.e. by the value of i_0. We agree accordingly that $i_0 = 0$ is to designate a standard number, and $i_0 = 1$ an order.

15.2 The remaining 31 units of a standard number express its binary digits and its sign. It is in the nature of all arithmetical operations, specifically because of the role of carry digits, that the binary digits of the numbers which enter into them must be fed in from right to left, i.e. those with the lowest positional values first. (This is so because the digits appear in a temporal succession and not simultaneously, cf. 7.1. The details are most simply evident in the discussion of the adder in 7.2.) The sign plays the role of the digit farthest left, i.e. of the highest positional value (cf. 8.1). Hence it comes last, i.e. $i_{31} = 0$ designates the + sign and $i_{31} = 1$ the − sign. Finally by 9.2 the binary point follows immediately after the sign digit, and the number ξ thus represented must be moved mod 2 into the interval −1, 1. That is $\xi = i_{31} i_{30} i_{29} \cdots i_1 = \sum_{v=1}^{31} i_v 2^{v-31} \pmod 2, -1 \leq \xi < 1$.

15.3 The remaining 31 units of an order, on the other hand, must express the nature of this order. The orders were classified in 14.1 into four classes (a)-(d), and these were subdivided further as follows: (a) in 11.4, (b) in 14.2, (b) and (c) in 14.3, 14.4, and the second remark in 14.5. Accordingly, the following complete list of orders obtains:

(α) Orders for CC to instruct CA to carry out one of its ten specific operations enumerated in 11.4. (This is (a) in 14.1.) We designate these operations by the numbers $0, 1, 2, \cdots, 9$ in the order in which they occur in 11.4, and thereby place ourselves into the position to refer to any one of them by its number $w = 0, 1, 2, \cdots, 9$, which is best given as a 4-digit binary number (cf. however, {}). Regarding the origin of the numbers which enter (as variables) into these operations and the disposal of the result, this should be said: According to 11.4, the former comes from I_{ca} and J_{ca} and the latter goes to O_{ca}, all in CA (cf. Figures 16, 17), J_{ca} is fed through I_{ca}, and I_{ca} is the original input and O_{ca} the final output of CA. The feeding into I_{ca} will be described in (β), (γ), (θ) below, the disposal from O_{ca} will be described in (δ), (ϵ), (θ) below.

Certain operations are so fast (they can be handled so as to consume only the duration of a minor cycle) that it is worthwhile to bypass O_{ca} when disposing of their result. (cf. {}.)

The provisions for clearing I_{ca} and J_{ca} were described in 11.4. Regarding the clearing of O_{ca} this ought to be said: It would seem natural to clear O_{ca} each time after its contents have been transferred into M (cf. below). There are, however, cases when it is preferable not to transfer out from O_{ca}, and not to clear the contents of O_{ca}. Specifically: In the discussion of the operation s in 11.3 it turned out to be necessary to hold in this manner in O_{ca} the result of a previous operation −. Alternatively, the previous operation might also be +, i, j, or even ×, (cf. there). Another instance: If a multiplication xy is carried out, with an O_{ca} which contains, say, z at the beginning of the operation, then actually $z + xy$ will form in O_{ca} (cf. the discussion of multiplication in 7.7). It may therefore be occasionally desirable to hold the result of an operation, which is followed by a multiplication, in O_{ca}. Formation of sums $\sum xy$ is one example of this.

We need therefore an additional digit $c = 0, 1$ to indicate whether O_{ca} should or should not be cleared after the operation. We let $c = 0$ express the former, and $c = 1$ the latter.

(β) Orders for CC to cause the transfer of a standard number from a definite minor cycle in M to CA. (This is (b) in 14.1, type (b') of 14.2.) The minor cycle is defined by the two indices μ, ρ (cf. the third remark in 14.5). The transfer into CA is, more precisely, one into I_{ca} (cf. (α) above).

(γ) Orders for CC to cause the transfer of a standard number which follows immediately upon the order, into CA. (This is the immediate transfer of the second remark in 14.5 in the variant which corresponds to (β) above.) It is simplest to consider a minor cycle containing a standard number (the kind analyzed in 15.2) as such an order per se. This modifies the statement (loc. cit.) somewhat: The standard number in question is next in the minor cycle following immediately upon a minor cycle which has just given an order to CC, then the number will automatically operate as an immediate transfer order of the type described. (cf. also the pertinent remarks in (ϵ) and in (ζ) below.) The transfer into CA is again one into I_{ca} (cf. (α) or (β) above).

(δ) Orders for CC to cause the transfer of a standard number from CA to a definite minor cycle in M. (This is (b) in 14.1, type (b'') in 14.2.) The minor cycle in M is defined by the two indices μ, ρ, as in (β) above. The transfer from CA is, more precisely, one from O_{ca}—this was discussed, together with the necessary explanations and qualifications, in (α) above.

(ϵ) Orders for CC to cause the transfer of a standard number from CA into the minor cycle which follows immediately upon the one containing this order. (This is the immediate transfer, cf. the second remark in 14.5, in the variant which corresponds to (δ) above.) The transfer from CA is again one from O_{ca} (cf. (α) or (δ) above).

In this case the CC connection passes from this transfer order on to the next minor cycle into which the standard number in question is just being sent. There would be no point in CC now obeying (γ), and sending this number back into CA—also, there might be timing difficulties. It is best, therefore, to except this case explicitly from the operation of (γ). i.e.: (γ) is invalid if it follows immediately upon an (ϵ).

(θ) Orders for CC to cause the transfer of a standard number from CA into CA. (This is an operation of CA, the usefulness of which we recognized in 11.2. Cf. also {}.) More precisely, from O_{ca} into I_{ca} (cf. (α) above).

(ζ) Orders for CC to transfer its own connection with M to a definite minor cycle (elsewhere) in M. (This is (c) in 14.1.) The minor cycle in M is defined by the two indices μ, ρ, as in (β) above.

Note that a (β) could be replaced by a (ζ), considering (γ). The only difference is that (ζ) is a permanent transfer, while (β) is a transient one. This may serve to place additional emphasis on the corresponding considerations of 14.3 and 14.4.

(η) Orders controlling the operation of the input and the output of the device (i.e. I of 2.7 and O of 2.8) (This is (d) in 14.1.) As indicated in 14.1, the discussion of these orders is better delayed (cf. {}).

15.4 Let us now compare the numbers of digits necessary to express these orders with the number of available digits in a minor cycle—31, as stated at the beginning of 15.3.

To begin with we have in (α)–(η) 8 types of order, to distinguish these from each other requires 3 digits. Next, the types (α)–(ζ) (we postpone (η), cf. above) have these requirements: (α) must specify the number w, i.e. 4 digits, plus the digit c—all together 5 digits. (β), as well as (δ) and (ζ), must specify the numbers μ and ρ, i.e. $8 + 5 = 13$ digits. (γ) is outside this category. (ϵ), as well as (θ), requires no further specifications.

Neither of these uses the 31 available digits very efficiently. Consequently we might consider putting several such orders into one minor cycle. On the other hand such a tendency to pool orders should be kept within very definite limits, for the following reasons.

First, pooling several orders into one minor cycle should be avoided, if it requires the simultaneous performance of several operations (i.e. violates the principle of 5.6.) Second, it should also be avoided if it upsets the timing of the operations. Third, the entire matter is usually not important from the point of view of the total memory capacity: Indeed, it reduces the number of those minor cycles only, which are used for logical instructions, i.e. for the purpose (b) in 2.4, and these represent usually only a small fraction of the total capacity of M (cf. (b) in 12.3 and {}). Hence the pooling of orders should rather be carried out from the point of view of simplifying the logical structure of the code.

15.5 These considerations discourage pooling several orders of the type (α)—besides this would often not be logically possible either, without intervening orders of the types (β)–(ζ). Combining two orders of the types (β), (δ), (ζ) is also dubious from the above points of view, besides it would leave only $31 - 3 - 13 - 13 = 2$ digits free, and this (although it could be increased by various tricks to 3) is uncomfortably low: It is advisable to conserve some spare capacity in the logical part of the code (i.e. in the orders), since later on changes might be desirable. (e.g. it may become advisable to increase the capacity of M, i.e. the number 256 of major cycles, i.e. the number 8 of digits of μ. For another reason cf. {}.

The best chance lies in pooling an operation order (α) with orders controlling the transfer of its variables into CA or the transfer of its result out of CA. Both types may involve 13 digit orders (namely (β) or (δ)), hence we cannot count on pooling (α) with more than one such order (cf. the above estimate plus the 5 digits required by (α)!). Now one (α) usually requires transferring two variables into CA, hence the simplest systematical procedure consists in pooling (α) with the disposal of its result. I.e. (α) with (δ) or (ϵ) or (θ). It should be noted that every (δ), (ϵ) (θ), i.e. transfer from CA, must be preceded by an (α), and every (β), (γ), i.e. transfer into CA, must be followed by an (α). Indeed, these transfers are always connected with an (α) operation, the only possible exception would be an M to M transfer, routed through (α), but even this involves an (α) operation (i or j in 11.4, cf. there and in 11.2). Consequently orders (δ), (ϵ), (θ) will always occur pooled with (α), and orders (β), (γ) will always occur alone. (α) too may occasionally occur alone: If the result of the operation ordered by (α) is to be held in O_{ca} (cf. the last part of (α) in 15.3), then it will usually not be necessary or desirable to dispose of this result in any other way (cf. the examples loc. cit.). We shall keep both possibilities open: There may or may not be an additional disposal of the result, and in the second case (α) will not be pooled with any disposal order. Orders (ζ) are of a sufficiently exceptional logical character, to justify that they too always occur alone.

Thus we have—if we disregard (γ), which is in reality a standard number—the 7 following types of orders: $(\alpha) + (\delta)$, $(\alpha) + (\epsilon)$, $(\alpha) + (\theta)$, (α), (β), (ζ), (η). They require $5 + 13 = 18$, 5, 5, 5, 13, 13 digits (we disregard (η), which will be discussed later) plus 3 digits to distinguish the types from each other, plus one digit ($i_0 = 1$) to express that an order is involved. Hence the totals are 22, 9, 9, 9, 17, 17 digits. This is an average efficiency of $\approx 50\%$ in utilizing the 32 digits of a minor cycle. This efficiency can be considered adequate, in view of the third remark of 15.4, and it leaves at the same time a comfortable spare capacity (cf. the beginning of 15.5).

15.6 We are now in the position to formulate our code. This formulation will be presented in the following manner:

We propose to characterize all possible minor cycles which may be used by the device. These are standard numbers and orders, already enumerated and described in 15.1–15.5. In the table which follows we will specify the four following things for each possible minor cycle: (I) The *type*, i.e. its relationship to the classification (α)–(η) of 15.3, and to the pooling procedures of 15.5; (II) The *meaning*, as described in 15.1–15.5; (III) The *short symbol*, to be used in verbal or written discussions of the code, and in particular in all further analyses of this paper, and when setting up problems for the device (cf. {}); (IV) The *code symbol*, i.e. the 32 binary digits $i_0, i_1, i_2, \ldots, i_{31}$

which correspond to the 32 units of the minor cycle in question. However, there will only be partial statements on this last point at this time, the precise description will be given later (cf. {}).

Regarding the numbers (binary integers) which occur in these symbols, we observe this: These numbers are μ, ρ, w, c. We will denote their binary digits (in the usual, left to right, order) by $u_7, \ldots, u_0; \rho_4, \ldots, \rho_0; w_3, \ldots, w_0; c$.

(I) Type	(II) Meaning	(III) Short Symbol	(IV) Code Symbol
			Minor cycle $I = (i_v) =$ $(i_0 i_1 i_2 \cdots i_{31})$
Standard Number or Order (γ)	Storage for the number defined by $\xi = i_{31} i_{30} \cdots i_1 = \sum_{v=1}^{31} i_v 2^{v-31} \pmod 2$ $-1 \le \xi < 1$. i_{31} is the sign: 0 for $+$, 1 for $-$. If CC is connected to this minor cycle, then it operates as an order, causing the transfer of ξ into I_{ca}. This does not apply however if this minor cycle follows immediately upon an order $w \to A$ or $wh \to A$.	Nξ	$i_0 = 0$
Order $(\alpha) + (\delta)$ ———— Order $(\alpha) + (\epsilon)$ ———— Order $(\alpha) + (\theta)$ ———— Order (α)	Order to carry out the operation w in CA and to dispose of the result. w is from the list of 11.4. These are the operations of 11.4, with their current numbers w.decimal and w.binary, and their symbols w: 	w.decimal	w.binary	w	w.decimal	w.binary	w
---	---	---	---	---	---
0	0000	+	5	0101	i
1	0001	−	6	0110	j
2	0010	×	7	0111	s
3	0011	÷	8	1000	db
4	0100	√	9	1001	bd | h means that the result is to be held in O_{ca}. $\to \mu\rho$ means that the result is to be transferred into the minor cycle ρ in the major cycle μ; $\to$ f, that it is to be transferred into the minor cycle immediately following upon the order ϵ; $\to$ A, that it is to be transferred into I_{ca}; no $\to$, that no disposal is wanted (apart from h).	w $\to \mu\rho$ or wh $\to \mu\rho$ ———— w $\to$ f or wh $\to$ f ———— w $\to$ A or wh $\to$ A ———— wh	$i_0 = 1$
Order (β)	Order to transfer the number in the minor cycle ρ in the major cycle μ into I_{ca}.	A $\leftarrow \mu\rho$	
Order (ζ)	Order to connect CC with the minor cycle ρ in the major cycle μ.	C $\leftarrow \mu\rho$	

Remark: Orders w (or wh) $\to \mu\rho$ (or f) transfer a standard number ξ from CA into a minor cycle. If this minor cycle is of the type Nξ (i.e. $i_0 = 0$), then it should clear its 31 digits representing ξ', and accept the 31 digits of ξ. If it is a minor cycle ending in $\mu\rho$ (i.e. $i_0 = 1$, order $w \to \mu\rho$ or $wh \to \mu\rho$ or A $\leftarrow \mu\rho$ or C $\leftarrow \mu\rho$), then it should clear only its 13 digits representing $\mu\rho$, and accept the last 13 digits of ξ!

COMPARISON CHART FOR EDVACS

	EDVAC I	EDVAC II	EDVAC III
Cost	Covered by current contract	Present contract plus $80,000	Present contract plus $180,000
Completion date	July 1947	October 1947	March 1948
Number notation	Binary	Decimal	Decimal
Digit capacity	32, binary (equiv. to 10, decimal)	10, decimal	7, decimal from 10^{-99} to 10^{99}
Handling of decimal point	Manual	Manual	Fully automatic
Automatic Calculator Check	No	Yes	Yes
Basic arith. oper.	$+, -, \times$, division to be programmed	$+, -, \times, \div$	$+, -, \times, \div$
Number of tubes in arith. organ	200	750	2000
No. of tubes in control	500	700	1000
No. of tubes in memory	700	800	1600
No. of tubes in input & output	200	300	400
Total tubes	1600[a]	2550[a]	5000[a]
High speed mem. cap.	1000 words[b]	1000 words[b]	4000 words[b]
Word length (pulses)	36	52	48
Time + -	36	52	144
Time ×	1150 μsec.	1040 μsec.	24-48 μsec.
Power consumption	15 KW	25 KW	60 KW

(a) Less power supplies which add about 200 tubes to each. The tube envelopes (not elements) are counted.
(b) A word consists of a group of pulses corresponding to an order or a number.